THIS PAGE:
Devils Tower, Devils Tower NM

ON THE COVER:
Devils Tower, Devils Tower NM

NPS Photos by: Deanna Greco

Devils Tower National Monument
Geologic Resource Evaluation Report

Natural Resource Report NPS/NRPC/GRD/NRR—2008/046

Geologic Resources Division
Natural Resource Program Center
P.O. Box 25287
Denver, Colorado 80225

September 2008

U.S. Department of the Interior
Washington, D.C.

The Natural Resource Publication series addresses natural resource topics that are of interest and applicability to a broad readership in the National Park Service and to others in the management of natural resources, including the scientific community, the public, and the NPS conservation and environmental constituencies. Manuscripts are peer-reviewed to ensure that the information is scientifically credible, technically accurate, appropriately written for the intended audience, and is designed and published in a professional manner.

Natural Resource Reports are the designated medium for disseminating high priority, current natural resource management information with managerial application. The series targets a general, diverse audience, and may contain NPS policy considerations or address sensitive issues of management applicability. Examples of the diverse array of reports published in this series include vital signs monitoring plans; "how to" resource management papers; proceedings of resource management workshops or conferences; annual reports of resource programs or divisions of the Natural Resource Program Center; resource action plans; fact sheets; and regularly-published newsletters.

Views, statements, findings, conclusions, recommendations and data in this report are solely those of the author(s) and do not necessarily reflect views and policies of the U.S. Department of the Interior, National Park Service. Mention of trade names or commercial products does not constitute endorsement or recommendation for use by the National Park Service.

Printed copies of reports in these series may be produced in a limited quantity and they are only available as long as the supply lasts. This report is also available online from the Geologic Resource Evaluation Program website (http://www2.nature.nps.gov/geology/inventory/gre_publications) and the Natural Resource Publication Management website (http://www.nature.nps.gov/publications/NRPM/index.cfm) or by sending a request to the address on the back cover.
Please cite this publication as:

Graham, J. 2008. Badlands National Park Geologic Resource Evaluation Report. Natural Resource Report NPS/NRPC/GRD/NRR—2008/046. National Park Service, Denver, Colorado.

NPS D-86, September 2008

Table of Contents

Attachment 1: Geologic Resource Evaluation Products CD

List of Figures

Executive Summary

This report accompanies the digital geologic map for Devils Tower National Monument in Wyoming, which the Geologic Resources Division produced in collaboration with its partners. It contains information relevant to resource management and scientific research.

Devils Tower National Monument has the distinction of being the nation's first national monument, established in 1906 by Theodore Roosevelt. The monolithic Devils Tower is world renown for its spectacular columnar jointing. At 1,546 m (5,070 ft) above mean sea level, Devils Tower rises 386 m (1,267 ft) above the Belle Fourche River and stands as the most widely recognized landmark of the northern Great Plains.

Geologic issues in Devils Tower National Monument include potential rockfalls from two rock units in the monument and high erosion rates for some of the sedimentary strata. The broad apron of talus surrounding Devils Tower attests to rockfall from failure along the fractures and joints that define the igneous columns of the Tower. Rockfalls also may occur by the spalling of rectangular blocks from cliffs of the Hulett Sandstone. Rockfalls may perpetuate landslides down the hill below the cliffs.

Permian, Triassic, and Jurassic sedimentary units of red, yellow, gray, and green shale; siltstone and sandstone; and white gypsum form the rolling hills and gentle slopes that surround Devils Tower. The shales and siltstones are poorly cemented and erode easily. Because the units are so soft, erosion may undercut buildings and roads constructed on these units.

Devils Tower is a bare mass of rock that rises abruptly from the surrounding grasslands and pine forests. The Tower is about 244 m (800 ft) in diameter at its base while its summit measures roughly 55 m (180 ft) from east to west and 90 m (300 ft) from north to south. The polygonal columns are one of the most striking features of Devils Tower. The larger columns taper from a basal 1.8–2.4 m (6–8 ft) in diameter to about 1.2 m (4 ft) at the top.

The origin of Devils Tower is presently debated. Some believe the tower is the remnant of a volcanic neck. Others believe the phonolite porphyry that comprises the Tower is the remnant of a laccolith or sill. Another view holds that the Tower is the remains of a lopolith; igneous material that once filled a shallow structural depression.

The Permian, Triassic and Jurassic sedimentary strata record a complex depositional history of the Black Hills region. Both marine and terrestrial rocks were deposited during several episodes of transgressive-regressive cycles. The late Cretaceous to Tertiary Laramide Orogeny resulted in the uplift of the Black Hills, the onset of erosion, and the emplacement of the igneous body that would become Devils Tower. In the late Tertiary and Quaternary, regional uplift followed by erosion by the Belle Fourche River and its tributaries resulted in the current topography of Devils Tower.

Introduction

The following section briefly describes the National Park Service Geologic Resource Evaluation Program and the regional geologic setting of Devils Tower National Monument.

Purpose of the Geologic Resources Evaluation Program

The Geologic Resource Evaluation (GRE) Program is one of 12 inventories funded under the NPS Natural Resource Challenge designed to enhance baseline information available to park managers. The program carries out the geologic component of the inventory effort from the development of digital geologic maps to providing park staff with a geologic report tailored to a park's specific geologic resource issues. The Geologic Resources Division of the Natural Resource Program Center administers this program. The GRE team relies heavily on partnerships with the U.S. Geological Survey, Colorado State University, state surveys, and others in developing GRE products.

The goal of the GRE Program is to increase understanding of the geologic processes at work in parks and provide sound geologic information for use in park decision making. Sound park stewardship relies on understanding natural resources and their role in the ecosystem. Geology is the foundation of park ecosystems. The compilation and use of natural resource information by park managers is called for in section 204 of the National Parks Omnibus Management Act of 1998 and in NPS-75, Natural Resources Inventory and Monitoring Guideline.

To realize this goal, the GRE team is systematically working towards providing each of the identified 270 natural area parks with a geologic scoping meeting, a digital geologic map, and a geologic report. These products support the stewardship of park resources and are designed for non-geoscientists. During scoping meetings the GRE team brings together park staff and geologic experts to review available geologic maps and discuss specific geologic issues, features, and processes.

The GRE mapping team converts the geologic maps identified for park use at the scoping meeting into digital geologic data in accordance with their innovative Geographic Information Systems (GIS) Data Model. These digital data sets bring an exciting interactive dimension to traditional paper maps by providing geologic data for use in park GIS and facilitating the incorporation of geologic considerations into a wide range of resource management applications. The newest maps come complete with interactive help files. As a companion to the digital geologic maps, the GRE team prepares a park-specific geologic report that aids in use of the maps and provides park managers with an overview of park geology and geologic resource management issues.

For additional information regarding the content of this report and up to date GRE contact information please refer to the Geologic Resource Evaluation Web site (http://www.nature.nps.gov/geology/inventory/).

Regional Information and Geologic Setting

Devils Tower National Monument, in northeast Wyoming, is the nation's the first national monument, established by Theodore Roosevelt in 1906 (fig. 1). Devils Tower is a steep sided igneous monolith recognized worldwide for a spectacular geologic feature known as columnar jointing (fig. 2). It is also the most widely known landmark of the northern Great Plains. Elevation at the relatively flat summit of Devils Tower is 1,560 m (5,117 ft) above sea level (Karner and Halvorson 1987, 1989; Kiver and Harris 1999). The top of the Tower measures about 55 m (180 ft) from east to west and about 91 m (300 ft) from north to south (Robinson 1956). Devils Tower rises about 386 m (1,267 ft) above the north-flowing Belle Fourche River, which is responsible for excavating the buried igneous feature and continues to cut away at its south flank.

The crystalline igneous rock that composes Devils Tower is classified as phonolite porphyry. Phonolite is a type of fine-grained igneous rock composed primarily of the mineral feldspar. A 'porphyry' is a rock that has coarse crystals surrounded by fine-grained material, or groundmass. The groundmass of fresh specimens is light- to dark-gray or greenish-gray and contains conspicuous crystals of white feldspar that are about 0.6–1.3 cm (0.25–0.50 in) in diameter and smaller very dark-green crystals of pyroxene, a group of dark rock-forming silicate minerals. Weathered surfaces appear light gray or brownish gray and lichens may give the phonolite a green, yellowish-green, or brown color.

An apron of talus (eroded blocks lying at the base of the cliff), landslide material, and the remnants of a large volume of alloclastic breccia (a coarse-grained sedimentary rock formed by volcanic processes) surround the Tower. Debris from the Tower and the Hulett Sandstone Member of the Jurassic Sundance Formation comprise the talus and landslide material. The talus sheet radiates outward from the tower about 335 m (1,100 ft). Near the base of the Tower, talus is about 46 m (150 ft) thick, but it thins rapidly away from the monolith (fig. 2) (Karner and Halvorson 1989). Talus fragments range from a few centimeters in diameter to large sections of the columns as much as 2.4 m (8 ft) in diameter and 7.6 m (25 ft) long (Robinson 1956). Within the talus sheet, three outcrops of phonolite may be radiating dikes (igneous intrusions shaped like a table top turned on edge) or part of the original uneroded igneous mass.

Red, yellow, green, or gray sedimentary rocks compose the hills in the vicinity of Devils Tower (fig. 3). These beds of sandstone, siltstone, shale, and gypsum are about 122 m (400 ft) thick. The oldest unit is the Triassic/Permian Spearfish Formation (fig. 4). The Spearfish Formation is overlain by Jurassic strata. Although no Cretaceous or Tertiary sedimentary rocks are exposed in Devils Tower National Monument, Cretaceous strata and the Oligocene White River Formation are present in the Missouri Buttes, smaller bodies of columnar-jointed igneous rock exposed northwest of Devils Tower (fig. 5) (Robinson 1956; Karner and Halvorson 1989).

On a regional scale, the sedimentary strata present in Devils Tower National Monument are gently folded into many small rolls, basins, and domes. Faults of small displacement locally cut these structures. The small folds are superimposed on a large dome that is collapsed in the middle (Robinson 1956). This broad dome is defined by sedimentary strata that are exposed 0.8–1.6 km (0.5–1 mi) from the Tower and that dip gently 2°–5° away from the Tower. Within about 600–900 m (2,000–3,000 ft) of the Tower, however, the strata reflect the dome's collapse by dipping 3°–5° inward to form a shallow structural basin.

Three faults are recognized in Devils Tower National Monument (Robinson 1956). Two of the faults cut the Hulett Sandstone west of the main road and west of the Tower. A third fault is in the northwestern side of the Tower near the Tower's base. The faults in the Hulett Sandstone are near vertical with displacements of less than 3 m (10 ft). The fault near the base of the Tower is a low-angle fault that trends northwesterly and dips 21° to the northeast.

Devils Tower is located on the northwest flank of the Black Hills, an uplift formed during the Cretaceous-Tertiary mountain-building episode called the Laramide Orogeny that occurred about 45–65 million years ago (Ma) (fig. 6). The Black Hills form a 105 by 200 km (125 by 65 mi) elliptical dome, or doubly plunging anticline, that is elongated in a north–south direction (Kiver and Harris 1999). This forested mountain range in southwest South Dakota and northeastern Wyoming covers approximately 2 million acres. Erosion has removed the Paleozoic and Mesozoic strata from the central axis of the dome, exposing Precambrian rocks that make up the core of the uplift. The younger sedimentary rocks of Paleozoic and Mesozoic age form concentric rings around the Precambrian core (fig. 6).

Park History

The earliest maps of this region named this structure "Bear Lodge," translated from the Cheyenne and Lakota Sioux's "Mateo Teepee" which means "Grizzly Bear Lodge" (Effinger 1934). In 1875, Colonel Richard Dodge led a U.S. Geological Survey expedition to the Black Hills. His interpreters misunderstood the Native American's description of the feature and translated it as "Bad God's Tower." Dodge reported it as Devils Tower and the name stuck. Since the tower figures strongly in the creation history of at least 20 Native American tribes, the name "Devils Tower" is offensive to many of them (Kiver and Harris 1999).

Early settlers were drawn to the area and Devils Tower became a special place for social gatherings and celebrations. In 1893, local ranchers William Rogers and Willard Ripley climbed to the top of the tower using 76-cm-long (30-in) stakes that they had pounded into a continuous crack that led to the summit. Portions of that stake ladder are still visible from the Tower Trail.

In 1906, shortly after Congress passed the Antiquities Act, Theodore Roosevelt established Devils Tower National Monument.

The first successful rock climb using mountaineering techniques was in 1937. In 1941, Jack Durrance led a group to the top to rescue George Hopkins who had parachuted onto the summit as a stunt (Kiver and Harris 1999). The Durrance route remains a popular climbing route.

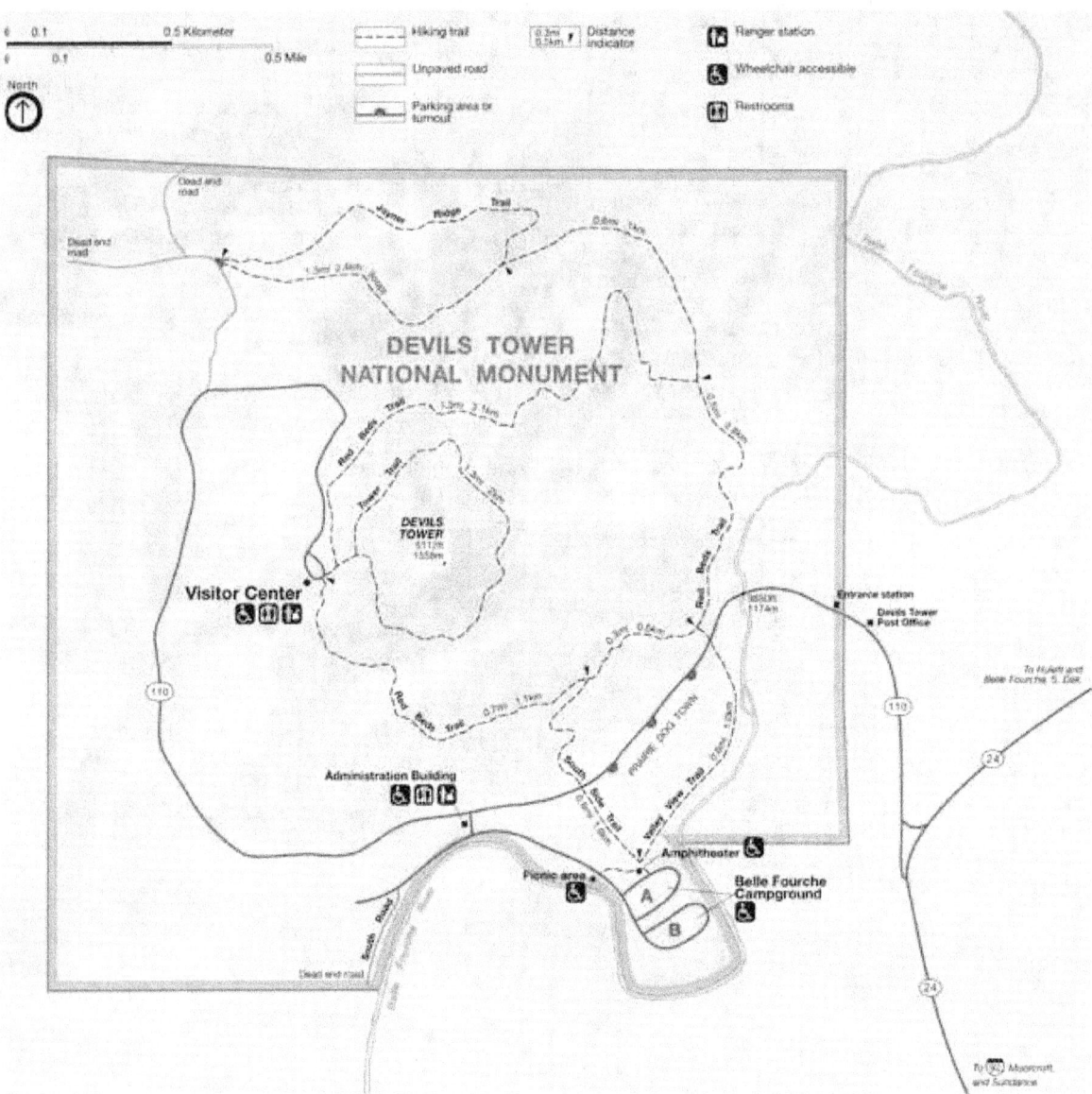

Figure 1. Location map of Devils Tower National Monument.

Figure 2. Devils Tower at Devils Tower National Monument. View to the east with the Belle Fourche River in the background. Note the columnar jointing and the relatively flat summit. An apron of talus, derived from the columns, extends outward from the base of the Tower. Photograph by Louis J. Maher, Jr., University of Wisconsin, available at http://www.geology.wisc.edu/~maher/air/air01.htm (access February 6, 2008).

System	Series	Formation, Unit or Member	Thickness in meters (feet)	Brief description
Quaternary		Undivided		Stream terrace deposits; alluvium; talus; landslide material
unconformity				
Tertiary		Phonolite porphyry		Dark-gray to black igneous rock
unconformity				
Jurassic	Upper	Sundance Formation Redwater Shale Member	12-55 (40-180)	Greenish-gray shale
		Sundance Formation Lak Member	11-20 (35-65)	Yellow, yellowish-brown, to pink calcareous sandstone & siltstone
		Sundance Formation Hulett Sandstone F Member	18-27 (60-90)	Yellow, massive calc. sandstone
		Sundance Formation Stockade Beaver Shale Mbr	18-24 (60-80)	Gray & gray-green shales with thin calcareous sandstones
unconformity				
	Middle	Gypsum Spring Formation	0-20 (0-65)	White massive gypsum with interbedded red mudstone
unconformity				
Triassic/ Permian		Spearfish Formation	183+ (600+)	Red to maroon siltstone & sandstone interbedded with shale

Figure 3. Generalized stratigraphic column for units exposed in Devils Tower National Monument from Robinson (1956) with the exception of the Spearfish Formation. Robinson considered the Spearfish Formation to be Triassic. However, since 1956, researchers have extended the Spearfish Formation into the Permian. In addition, the Lak Member of the Sundance Formation may be part of the Hulett Sandstone Member (Jack Epstein, USGS, written communication, January 25, 2008).

Figure 4. Spearfish Formation in the Black Hills region. Red beds are siltstone and sandstone; white is gypsum. Photo courtesy of Dr. Steven Dutch, Natural and Applied Sciences, University of Wisconsin – Green Bay, available at http://www.uwsp.edu/geo/projects/geoweb/participants/dutch/VTrips/BHStrat.HTM (access February 4, 2008).

Figure 5. Devils Tower at Devils Tower National Monument. View to the northwest with the Missouri Buttes in the left background. Missouri Buttes are smaller bodies of columnar-jointed igneous intrusions. Photograph by Louis J. Maher, Jr., University of Wisconsin, available at http://www.geology.wisc.edu/~maher/air/air01.htm (access February 6, 2008).

Figure 6. Diagram of the Black Hills dome showing progressively younger sedimentary rock layers ringing the central Precambrian core. Devils Tower National Monument lies within the northwest flank of the Black Hills. Modified from Strahler, 1960.

Geologic Issues

A Geologic Resource Evaluation scoping session was held for Devils Tower National Monument on June 12, 2002, to discuss geologic resources, address the status of geologic mapping, and assess resource management issues and needs. This section synthesizes the scoping results, in particular those issues that may require attention from resource managers.

The geologic issues section addresses geologic issues as they affect the ecosystem, their importance to park management, and the extent to which they are influenced by human activities.

Rock Climbing

The vertical cracks and columns at Devils Tower have made the Monument a world-renowned site for crack climbing. Over 4,000 climbers visit Devils Tower each year, and the tower now has about 220 named routes. Including the famed Durrance Route, the most popular climbing route at the Monument, highlighted in Steve Roper and Allen Steck's book, 50 classic climbs in North America (fig. 7). By 1995, about 600 metal bolts had been embedded in the rock along with several hundred metal pitons, and activities from numerous climbers through the spring to fall climbing season had affected nesting raptors, soil, vegetation, the integrity of the rock, the area's natural quiet, and the rock's physical appearance.

Devils Tower is also a sacred site to several Native American peoples of the northern plains. Some Native Americans complained that climbers on the sacred butte and the placement of bolts in the rock adversely impacted their traditional activities and seriously impaired the spiritual quality of the site.

To address these issues, park staff developed a final climbing management plan (FCMP) that focuses on the following objectives:

- Preserve and protect the monument's natural and cultural resources for present and future generations,

- Manage recreational climbing on the tower,

- Increase visitor awareness of Native American beliefs and traditional cultural practices at Devils Tower, and

- Provide the monument with a guide for managing climbing use that is consistent with NPS management policies and other management plans at Devils Tower National Monument.

The FCMP decreased the physical impact to Devils Tower by eliminating the placement of new bolts or fixed pitons although replacement of existing bolts and fixed pitons is allowed. In 1995, the NPS implemented a voluntary June closure to climbing on Devils Tower in honor of the culturally significant month of June, and monument staff began interpreting the cultural significance of Devils Tower to all visitors. In the spring, NPS personnel identify falcon nest sites so that climbing routes within view of the nest site, or approximately 50 m

(160 ft) on either side of the nest, are closed for the duration of the nesting season.

Rehabilitation of access trails and summit trails helped repair soil and vegetation damage. The FCMP has significantly increased protection for natural resources and enhanced visitor experience by a more diverse and balanced interpretive program. This plan is currently being revised and is expected to continue the responsible management of climbing in the monument.

Rockfall

Potential rockfalls may occur from two rock units in the monument: the sandstone cliffs of the Hulett Member of the Sundance Formation and the phonolite porphyry of the Devils Tower (Robinson 1956). Portions of the Hulett sandstone cliff that surrounds the Tower may break off into rectangular blocks. These blocks form talus at the base of the cliff and locally cause large landslides on the hill below the cliffs (Robinson 1956). These blocks of sandstone range in size from a few inches to many feet in diameter.

The broad apron of phonolite porphyry talus surrounding the Tower is a result of rockfall caused by failure along the fractures and joints that define the igneous columns. The column fragments measure from a few inches in diameter to as much as 2.4 m (8 ft) in diameter and 7.6 m (25 ft) long.

The Monument is a popular climbing destination. The potential for injury from falling rocks is safety concern for climbers on the tower as well as visitors using the Tower Trail. There have been no recorded injuries from rockfall along the Tower Trail, and rockfall injuries to climbers are uncommon. The diligent promotion of climbing safety by the Climbing Rangers at Devils Tower National Monument through education and awareness programs deserves credit for this astounding safety record.

No major rockfalls from the Tower have occurred in recent history. However, the Leaning Column is on the first pitch of the Durrance route has raised concerns. More than 4,000 people climb Devils Tower annually. The Durrance route sees a large portion of the climbing traffic with about 1,100 climbers ascending each year. In 2004, a tower guide reported that the column was moving. In response, the U.S. Geological Survey conducted an analysis of the column in June 2005 (Harp and Lindsay 2005).

According to the study, the column, at 26 feet long, has an estimated mass of 41 tons (82,000 pounds) (fig's. 7–8). It is composed of three vertically stacked fractured segments. The Leaning Column is in linear contact with the underlying columnar pedestal, and the top edge of the column is in point contact with an adjacent column. The column contains two primary axis points at its lower and upper contacts. Due to the precarious nature of the two contact points, the stability of the column is in question. The column may remain in place for years or even hundreds of years. If new fractures are detected at the lower contact of the column with the pedestal, this is an indication of an unstable and deteriorating condition. It is likely that more fractures will occur to the column or to the one that now supports it. This will eventually lead to failure of the pedestal and/or toppling of the column (Harp and Lindsay 2005).

Under a failure scenario, rockfall will impact the large flat bench at the base of the tower in the area directly south and west of the Tower Trail and adjacent to the steel viewing tubes. Any climber or hiker in the boulder field could be harmed by direct impact with falling rocks or from flying rock fragments. Failure could also lead to destabilization of other columns or rocks in the path of the event (Harp and Lindsay 2005).

Currently, Devils Tower National Monument Climbing Rangers are monitoring the leaning column for signs of fresh phonolite rock surfaces that would indicate spalling failures. In addition, they have noted and are keeping a photo documentation record of any fractures or changes in the column. To better detect any new changes, park staff have painted the surface of the column.

Mitigation of rockfall hazards generally can be dealt with in three ways: avoidance, stabilization, or removal. The simplest way to mitigate rockfall hazards is to avoid areas prone to rockfall. If an area is to be used, there are several ways that the hazard can be decreased. Rocks can be stabilized by bolting, cementing or in some cases removal of unstable rocks. Bolting and cementing are expensive, require periodic maintenance and seldom completely eliminate the hazard. Stabilization is usually only a short-term solution. While removal of all potentially unstable rocks is not possible, in some cases, individual rocks can be removed to eliminate an immediate hazard. It is crucial to assess and monitor potentially unstable rocks so that appropriate management action can be pursued.

Redbed erosion rates

The Permian, Triassic, and Jurassic red siltstone and sandstone sedimentary strata form rolling hills and gentle slopes because the units are poorly cemented and weather easily. The Administration Building and Visitor Center are constructed on the Redwater Shale Member of the Sundance Formation. Route 10 traverses several shale and siltstone units that are common to the formations in the monument. Because these units are so soft, the construction of new buildings and maintenance of existing buildings may be impacted and undercut by erosion because the units are so soft.

Past erosion processes that included heavy runoff from hillsides caused silt to be deposited in drainage ditches, plugging culverts associated with the main entrance road (Route 10). With culverts plugged, water and debris flowed over the road. The preferred alternative (3) of the General Management Plan (NPS 2001) addresses the redbed erosion issue. The preferred alternative proposes abandonment of two of the existing culverts (plugged and buried in place) and redirection of runoff into a new paved drainage swale running along the edge of the road, then under the road via two new trench drains and one existing culvert that will be maintained in place (fig. 9). The project is designed to create a landform that more closely resembles natural conditions (Jim Cheatham, Chief of Resource Management, Devils Tower National Monument, written communication, March 30, 2006).

Paleontology

Paleontological resources have not been fully assessed at Devils Tower National Monument but are considered a relatively minor resource management concern (Jim Cheatham, Chief of Resource Management, Devils Tower National Monument, written communication, March 30, 2006). Clams, oysters, belemnites (squid), and other marine fossils are known from the Redwater Shale Member of the Sundance Formation, but no fossils have been found in the Spearfish or Gypsum Spring Formations in the monument.

In 1997, excavation work for the new sewage disposal system yielded subsurface belemnites. Surface deposits of ammonites and belemnites are also known from three areas. Monument staff only casually monitor these sites, as the threat of theft is low (Jim Cheatham, Chief of Resource Management, Devils Tower National Monument, written communication, March 30, 2006). The best exposures of the Redwater Shale Member in the area are on Fossil Hill, northwest of the monument (Robinson 1956).

Gypsum karst

Although currently not an issue at Devils Tower National Monument, gypsum karst presents geological and engineering problems in the Black Hills. Gypsum is found in four stratigraphic units in the Black Hills of South Dakota and Wyoming: the Pennsylvanian/Permian Minnelusa Formation, the Permian/Triassic Opeche and Spearfish Formations, and the Jurassic Gypsum Spring Formation. Of these, the Spearfish Formation and the Gypsum Spring Formation are exposed in Devils Tower National Monument.

In South Dakota, dissolution of gypsum in the Spearfish and Gypsum Spring Formations has resulted in collapse and formation of many sinkholes in several areas that are presently undergoing urban development (Davis and Beaver 2002; Epstein 2002, 2003). Evidence of subsidence includes sinkholes over 18 m (60 ft) deep that have opened up over the last several decades, collapse in water wells and natural springs, and fresh circular scarps surrounding shallow depressions. As development increases in the Black Hills, it may be beneficial to consider processes involved in the formation of gypsum karst as part of land-use planning.

Figure 7. Devils Tower National Monument Climbing Rangers ascend the leaning column on the classic Durrance Climbing route. Photograph by NPS Geologist Deanna Greco (2008).

Figure8. Devils Tower as viewed from the north. Note the position of the leaning column half way up in the center of this photo. Photograph by NPS Geologist Deanna Greco (2008).

A)

B)

Figure 9. Culverts along Route 10, Devils Tower National Monument. A) Culvert scheduled to be abandoned under General Management Plan Alternative 3, the preferred alternative. B) Culvert to be maintained in Alternative 3. Photographs courtesy of Jim Cheatham, Chief of Resource Management, Devils Tower National Monument.

Geologic Features and Processes

This section describes the most prominent and distinctive geologic features and processes in Devils Tower National Monument.

This section provides a descriptive list of the most prominent and unique features and processes in the monument.

Devils Tower

Devils Tower is the reason that President Teddy Roosevelt established the monument. This bare mass of rock rises abruptly from the surrounding grasslands and pine forests and is one of the most conspicuous geologic features of the Black Hills region (fig. 10). At its base, the Tower is about 244 m (800 ft) in diameter. The steep sides rise nearly vertically for about 12–30 m (40–100 ft) before sloping more gently to form a narrow bench. Above the bench, the sides again rise steeply, at angles of 75° to over 85°, to within about 30 m (100 ft) of the summit. At this point, the angle becomes less steep and the top edge of the Tower is somewhat rounded. In all, the Tower extends vertically about 183 m (600 ft) to an almost flat summit that measures roughly 55 m (180 ft) from east to west and 90 m (300 ft) from north to south (Robinson 1956).

The phonolite porphyry that comprises Devils Tower appears light gray or brownish gray on weathered surfaces but fresh samples show a light- to dark-gray or greenish-gray very fine-grained groundmass in which coarser crystals of white feldspar can be seen. These feldspar crystals range from about 0.6–1.2 cm (0.25–0.50 in) in diameter.

Columnar Jointing

The world-renowned polygonal columns are one of the most striking features of Devils Tower (fig. 7). In the middle part of the Tower, the columns are bounded by well-developed smooth joints, but as the columns taper upward, the joints between them may be wavy and some of the columns unite. Cross-fractures in the upper part of the Tower form many small irregularly shaped blocks.

The fractures are about 120° to each other and form 4 and 6 sided columns. The larger columns measure 1.8–2.4 m (6–8 ft) in diameter at their base and taper gradually upward to about 1.2 m (4 ft) at the top. In the central and upper parts of Devils Tower, the columns are almost vertical. However, they flare out at the bench about 30 m (100 ft) above the base, and they are nearly horizontal on the southwest side. Several columns may join to form a larger, less distinct column that merges with the massive base where the columns flare out.

Columnar joints form when shallow igneous bodies quickly cool. The fractures are a result of differential contraction during cooling because solidified rock requires less volume than molten rock.

Igneous bodies cool from the surface downward and from the periphery inward. This process produced the series of joints that parallels the circumference of the igneous mass and the set of vertical radial cracks that are perpendicular to the peripheral jointing (Karner and Halvorson 1989; Kiver and Harris 1999). As marginal cooling continued, horizontal columnar joints formed and eventually curved upward as vertical temperature gradients became greater than horizontal temperature gradients (fig. 9).

Origin of Devils Tower

The origin of the magma and the original shape of the igneous body now called Devils Tower has been a source of debate since geologists examined the structure in 1875. Carpenter (1888) originally proposed that Devils Tower was a volcanic-neck remnant, part of an ancient volcano that remained filled with magma following an eruption. He proposed that the magma cooled and contracted to form the columnar jointing seen today. The volcanic-neck hypothesis is still favored by many geologists (Dutton and Schwartz 1936; Halvorson 1980; Karner and Halvorson 1987).

Because phonolite porphyry fragments are so extensively strewn about on and in stream terrace deposits, other geologists believe that Devils Tower and Missouri Buttes, a mass of phonolite about 6.4 km (4 mi) northwest of Devils Tower, are remnants of a laccolith or sill (Jagger 1901; Darton 1909). The vent of this laccolith is thought to be under either Missouri Buttes (Jagger 1901) or Devils Tower (Darton 1909).

Robinson (1956) proposed that Devils Tower is an intrusive igneous body, such as a small pluton, and not the remnant of a volcano. He thinks that the Tower was never much larger in diameter than its present base, and that it is connected to a sill or laccolith type body at a depth of 300+ m (1,000+ ft). He based this hypothesis on the following observations:

- Recent erosion has exposed the present Tower. When intruded, it was surrounded and probably covered by several hundred feet of sedimentary rock.

- The mineral composition and texture are more typical of shallow igneous rocks formed at depth than extrusive rocks.

- No evidence of extrusive igneous activity has been found in the surrounding area.

- Missouri Buttes and Devils Tower have the same composition so they probably were derived from a common magma, possibly the magma of a large intrusive body, such as a laccolith or sill.

- A well drilled about 2.4 km (1.5 mi) southwest of Missouri Buttes encountered rock similar to both

Devils Tower and Missouri Buttes at about 430 m (1400 ft) below the base of Missouri Buttes. The rock in the drill hole probably represents an intrusive body, rather than the Precambrian basement, because the thickness of the sedimentary rocks in this area is normally much greater than this depth.

- The amount of talus, slope wash, or terrace gravel derived from Devils Tower and Missouri Buttes is relatively small, suggesting that the igneous bodies have not been extensively eroded. Therefore, the original igneous bodies were not much larger than what is presently exposed.

- Columnar jointing is common in igneous bodies intruded at relatively shallow depths.

- Both Devils Tower and Missouri Buttes lie in shallow structural depressions.

A fourth hypothesis suggests that the depression formed when rising magma encountered groundwater near Earth's surface, producing an explosion crater that later filled with lava or hot pyroclastic material that welded together, cooled, and contracted into columnar-jointed rock (Kiver and Harris 1999). This hypothesis suggests that Devils Tower had a very violent past and that erosion has removed most of the basin fill material. Only the thickest part of the igneous fill remains in the structure called Devils Tower.

Vertical columns form where heat is lost mostly to the atmosphere, or to the rock surface above or a flat surface below. More horizontal or inclined columns tend to form where heat is mostly lost to the surrounding vent or basin walls. Either a volcanic neck, shallow intrusion, or a sloping basin surface could account for the nearly vertical columns in the center of Devils Tower and the outward flaring columns elsewhere around the base. Thus, researchers continue to debate which hypothesis is correct.

While all of the origin hypotheses explain most of the observed features, no hypothesis explains all of the observed geologic data. No evidence of extrusive rock or phonolite debris occurs in the nearby White River sediments that were deposited in the Oligocene only a few million years after the Devils Tower rock crystallized, yet the vertical columns flaring outward at the base are similar to the columnar-jointing patterns that occur in known volcanic necks (Robinson 1998; Kiver and Harris 1999). The large crystals of feldspar in the phonolite suggest a slower rate of cooling that would occur with slightly deeper burial rather than the rapid cooling associated with a lava- or pyroclastic-debris-filled explosion crater at Earth's surface.

However Devils Tower formed, erosion by the Belle Fourche River and its tributaries, combined with mass-wasting weathering processes such as landslides, account for much of the topographic expression of the tower. The total thickness of Mesozoic strata that covered the Jurassic Redwater Shale Member of the Sundance Formation, the youngest sedimentary unit exposed in the monument, prior to the emplacement of the Tower is unknown, but the average total thickness of the overlying units is 504 m (1,652 ft). Erosion rates would have been variable, with faster rates of erosion occurring in the shales and less resistant strata of the Cretaceous-aged Bell Fourche Shale, Mowry Shale, and Skull Creek Shale and the Upper Jurassic Morrison Formation. More deeply weathered rock is exposed in the upper 45 m (150 ft) of Devils Tower than in the lower section, suggesting a longer exposure to weathering processes (Kiver and Harris 1999). Erosion may have slowed as resistant sandstones in the Cretaceous-aged Newcastle Sandstone and Fall River Formation were slowly removed. Wetter climates in the Pleistocene (Ice Age) also may have resulted in more frequent flood-swollen streams that contributed to periods of more intense erosion.

Figure 10. Devils Tower. Note the flat summit, vertical columnar jointing, and curved columns at the base of the Tower. Photograph from Harp and Lindsay (2005).

Map Unit Properties

This section identifies characteristics of map units that appear on the Geologic Resource Evaluation digital geologic map of Devils Tower National Monument. The accompanying table is highly generalized and is provided for background purposes only. Ground-disturbing activities should not be permitted or denied on the basis of information in this table.

Geologic maps facilitate an understanding of Earth, its processes, and the geologic history responsible for its formation. Hence, the geologic map for Devils Tower National Monument informed the "Geologic History," "Geologic Features and Processes," and "Geologic Issues" sections of this report. Geologic maps are essentially two-dimensional representations of complex three-dimensional relationships. The various colors on geologic maps represent rocks and unconsolidated deposits. Bold lines that cross and separate the color patterns mark structural features such as faults and folds. Point symbols indicate features such as dipping strata, sample localities, mine features, wells, and cave openings.

Incorporation of geologic data into a geographic information system (GIS) increases the utility of geologic maps and clarifies spatial relationships to other natural resources and anthropogenic features. Geologic maps are indicators of water resources because they show which rock units are potential aquifers and are useful for finding seeps and springs. Geologic maps do not show soil types and are not soil maps, but they do show parent material, a key factor in soil formation. Furthermore, resource managers have used geologic maps to make correlations between geology and biology; for instance, geologic maps have served as tools for locating threatened and endangered plant species.

Although geologic maps do not show where future earthquakes will occur, the presence of a fault indicates past movement and possible future seismic activity. Geologic maps will not show where the next landslide, rockfall, or volcanic eruption will occur, but mapped deposits show areas that have been susceptible to such geologic hazards. Geologic maps do not show archaeological or cultural resources, but past peoples may have inhabited or been influenced by various geomorphic features that are shown on geologic maps: alluvial terraces may preserve artifacts, and inhabited alcoves may occur at the contact between two rock units.

Geologic features and processes often occur in or can be restricted to a particular stratigraphic unit (group, formation, or member). For example, the Hulett Sandstone Member of the Sundance Formation forms a cliff that nearly encircles Devils Tower and the Gypsum

Spring Formation is known for beds of massive white gypsum.

The features and properties of the geologic units in the following table correspond to the accompanying digital geologic data. Map units are listed from youngest to oldest. Please refer to the geologic time scale (fig. 11) for the age associated with each time period. This table highlights characteristics of map units such as susceptibility to hazards; the occurrence of fossils, cultural resources, mineral resources, and caves; and the suitability as habitat or for recreational use. Not all of the map units in this table are present in Devils Tower National Monument. The following are source data for the GRE digital geologic map:

Robinson, C. S. 1956. *Geologic Map of Devils Tower National Monument, Wyoming.* Scale 1:48,000. U.S. Geological Survey Bulletin 1021-I. Reston, VA: U.S. Geological Survey.

Izett, Glen A. 1963. *Geologic Map of the Storm Hill Quadrangle, Wyoming.* Scale 1:24,000. U.S. Geological Survey. Miscellaneous Geologic Investigations Map I-372. Reston, VA: U.S. Geological Survey.

Mapel, W.J., C.S. Robinson, and P.K. Theobald. 1959. *Geologic and structure contour map of the northern and western flanks of the Black Hills, Wyoming, Montana, and South Dakota.* Scale 1:96,000. U.S. Geological Survey Oil and Gas Investigations Map OM-191. Reston, VA: U.S. Geological Survey.

Using ESRI ArcGIS software, the Geologic Resource Evaluation team created a digital geologic map from these sources. GRE digital geologic-GIS map products include data in ESRI shapefile and coverage GIS formats, FGDC metadata, a Windows HelpFile that contains all of the ancillary map information and graphics, and an ESRI ArcMap map document file that easily displays the map with appropriate symbology.

GRE digital geologic data are included on the attached CD and are available through the NPS Data Store (http://science.nature.nps.gov/nrdata/).

Map Unit Properties Table

Age	Map Unit (symbol)	Unit Description	Topographic Expression	Erosion Resistance	Paleontological Resources	Mineral Resources	Cultural Resources	Hazards	Suitability for Development	Other Geological Significance
QUATERNARY	Unconsolidated material (Qta, Qal, Qt, Ql, Qtp, Qls)	Qts: stream terrace deposits & alluvium, undifferentiated. Gravel, sand, silt, & mud. Stream deposits (alluvium) found in valleys of small streams around the Tower & in the valley of the Belle Fourche R., that cuts across the monument's SE corner. NE of the Belle Fourche R., between the river & the main road, is terrace cut into the Spearfish Fm. Qal: alluvium – sand, silt, & gravel Qt: terrace alluvium – sand, silt, & gravel Qtp: talus & landslide material Qls: talus & landslide material, chiefly Hulet Sandstone	Terraces & floodplains; talus slopes	Alluvium: low; Talus: high	None	Sand & Gravel	None documented	Flash flooding	Easily eroded; unstable foundation	None
TERTIARY	White River Formation (Twr)	Light-gray & light brown medium- to coarse-grained friable sandstone & conglomeratic sandstone; locally contains calcium carbonate cement. Locally thick bedded; unconformable lower contact. Thickness averages 9 m (30 ft), range 0.15 m (0-50 ft).	Forms slopes & some ragged ledges in area	Not exposed in Devils Tower NM	Early Oligocene brontothere tooth fragment found in gravel pit N of Devils Tower NM (NW¼ sec. 27, T55N, R65W)	Not exposed in Devils Tower NM	Not exposed in Devils Tower NM	Not exposed in Devils Tower NM	Not exposed in Devils Tower NM	None
					Unconformity					
TERTIARY	Phonolite porphyry (Tp)	Conspicuous crystals of white feldspar in light- to dark-gray or greenish-gray very fine-grained groundmass. Feldspar commonly about 0.6-1.2 cm (0.25-0.5 in) in diameter. Weathers to light gray or brownish gray. Under the microscope, the feldspar is crudely zoned, untwinned, & altered alkali feldspar (anorthoclase). Smaller dark-green pyroxene crystals are clinopyroxene, either aegirite or aegirite-augite. Similar in composition to the igneous rocks at Missouri Buttes.	Devils Tower	High	None	Feldspar (anorthoclase)	Most widely known landmark of the Northern Great Plains	Rockfall & landslide potential	Poor; many fractures; popular rock climbing routes	World renown columnar jointing
					Regional Unconformity					
LOWER CRETACEOUS	Belle Fourche Shale (Kb)	Dark-gray to black shale with numerous dark purplish-red weathering siderite concretions in lower part, & several beds of light-gray- & yellow-weathering limestone concretions in middle & upper parts; several beds of bentonite (altered volcanic ash). Not exposed in Devils Tower NM. Thickness: 210-240 m (700-800 ft).	Not exposed in Devils Tower NM	Low	Not exposed in Devils Tower NM	Siderite; Bentonite	Not exposed in Devils Tower NM	Bentonite	Bentonite may cause problems	Local commercial deposits of bentonite
LOWER CRETACEOUS	Mowry Shale (Km)	Dark-gray siliceous shale, weathers light gray; many thin bentonite beds. Thickness: 61-76 m (200-250 ft). Not exposed in Devils Tower NM.	Not exposed in Devils Tower NM	Low; Not in Devils Tower NM	Numerous fish scales along shale partings	Not exposed in Devils Tower NM	Not exposed in Devils Tower NM	Bentonite	Bentonite may cause problems	Remnants of an ancient sea floor
LOWER CRETACEOUS	Newcastle Sandstone (Knc)	Discontinuous beds of light-gray sandstone siltstone & dark-gray carbonaceous shale or claystone; a few beds of impure lignite & bentonite. Gradational lower contact. Thin to thick bedded; ripple marks; low-angle cross stratification. Thickness varies within short distances, but averages 11-12 m (35-40 ft). Not exposed in Devils Tower NM.	Forms slopes with some prominent ledges	Higher than shale; lower than phonolite	Not exposed in Devils Tower NM	Not exposed in Devils Tower NM	Not exposed in Devils Tower NM	Not exposed in Devils Tower NM	Prominent joints in sandstone & siltstone beds.	Not exposed in Devils Tower NM
LOWER CRETACEOUS	Skull Creek Shale (Ksc)	Slightly silty black shale with a few ferruginous siltstone, siderite, & cone-in-cone concretions; fissile to subfissile. Gradational lower contact. Thinly laminated. Thickness averages 76 m (250 ft). Not exposed in Devils Tower NM.	Forms gentle slopes	Low	Fragmentary plesiosaur bone found in lower part of formation	Not exposed in Devils Tower NM	Not exposed in Devils Tower NM	Not exposed in Devils Tower NM	Not exposed in Devils Tower NM	Remnants of an ancient sea floor
LOWER CRETACEOUS	Fall River Formation (Kr)	Gray to light-brown very fine grained thin- to thick-bedded sandstone with a few gray to light-brown silty claystone & clayey siltstone beds in upper part; gray to light-brown thinly laminated carbonaceous clayey siltstone & silty claystone layered with very fine to fine-grained sandstone in lower part. Unconformable lower contact. Thin to thick bedded; even bedded, locally lenticular, ripple marks; low-angle cross-stratification; sandstone bars & channel-fill deposits. Thickness avg 40 m (130 ft), range 37-44 m (120-145 ft). Not exposed in Devils Tower NM.	Forms ledges & cliffs separated by moderately steep slopes	Relatively high	Trails & tubes of soft-bodied organisms	Uranium	Not exposed in Devils Tower NM	Not exposed in Devils Tower NM	Prominent joints in sandstone & some siltstone beds	Locally contains disseminated uranium minerals
					Unconformity					
LOWER CRETACEOUS	Lakota Formation (Kl)	Variegated sandy claystone & clayey sandstone, gray dense siltstone, lenticular gray to light-brown sandstone & conglomeratic sandstone; contains highly polished pebbles of vari-colored chert, red & white quartzite, & white quartz. Unconformable lower contact, but locally gradational. No apparent fractures or joints. Thin- to thick-bedded, locally massive; rare ripple marks; low- to high-angle, medium-scale tabular & lenticular cross-stratification; lenticular sandstones common. Thickness avg 55 m (180 ft), range 35-79 m (115-260 ft). Not exposed in Devils Tower NM.	Forms moderately steep slopes with a few ledges and cliffs	Relatively high	Marine invertebrate fossil debris in polished pebbles & cobbles (Psozronax of Pennsylvanian or Permian age; Favosites sp. of Late Ordovician to Devonian age)	Uranium minerals	Not exposed in Devils Tower NM	Not exposed in Devils Tower NM	Not exposed in Devils Tower NM	Locally contains disseminated uranium minerals
					Regional Unconformity					

Age	Map Unit (symbol)	Unit Description	Topographic Expression	Erosion Resistance	Paleontological Resources	Mineral Resources	Cultural Resources	Hazards	Suitability for Development	Other Geological Significance
UPPER JURASSIC	Fuson & Lakota Formations, undifferentiated (Kfu)	Light yellowish-gray to white fine- to coarse-grained sandstone & conglomeratic sandstone; irregularly layered with red, green, yellow, gray, & black claystone; thickness variable within short distances. Thickness: 18-67 m (60-220 ft). Not exposed in Devils Tower NM.	Not exposed in Devils Tower NM	Not exposed in Devils Tower NM	Not exposed in Devils Tower NM	Coal	Not exposed in Devils Tower NM	Not exposed in Devils Tower NM	Not exposed in Devils Tower NM	Locally contains coal beds near base
	Morrison Formation (Jm)	Green, greenish gray, & grayish-red structureless limy claystone & slightly sandy claystone with a few thin discontinuous light-gray limestone & sandstone beds; locally consists entirely of light-gray very fine-grained sandstone that weathers to rounded knobs. Gradational lower contact. No apparent fractures or joints. Thin- to thick-bedded sandstone, lenticular & massive, rare ripple marks; low-angle medium-scale lenticular cross-stratification. Thickness avg 24 m (80 ft), range 0-30 m (0-100 ft). Not exposed in Devils Tower NM.	Weathers to rounded knobs & grass-covered slopes	Relatively low	Locally contains ostracodes, gastropods, & vertebrate remains	Not exposed in Devils Tower NM	Not exposed in Devils Tower NM	Not exposed in Devils Tower NM	Not exposed in Devils Tower NM	At Barlow Canyon Dome locally truncated by angular unconformity at base of Lakota Fm
	Sundance Fm.: Redwater Shale Member (Jsr)	Greenish-gray shale with thin discontinuous fossiliferous sandy limestone & limy siltstone beds in upper part; topmost bed is orange-brown limy siltstone. Gradational lower contact. No apparent fractures or joints. Thin-bedded limestone; ripple marks common in topmost sandstone beds. Thickness avg 52 m (170 ft), range 12-55 m (40-180 ft). Jsls: fossiliferous limestone beds in the upper part of the Redwater Shale Member	Forms grass-covered slopes; encircles Devils Tower; mostly covered by talus	Low	Fragments of marine invertebrates: ammonites, belemnites (squids), crinoid stems, & pelecypods (clams & oysters)	None documented	Unknown	None documented	Easily scarred by off-road vehicles; erosion potential from development	Best exposures are on Fossil Hill, NW of Devils Tower, & in NW corner of the monument.
	Sundance Fm.: Lak Member (Jsl)	Yellow to pink siltstone & very fine-grained sandstone & siltstone. Minor thin gray-green sandy shale partings. Poorly cemented. Gradational lower contact. No apparent fractures or joints. Thin-bedded sandstone in lower part. Thickness averages 14 m (45 ft), range 11-20 m (35-65 ft).	Weathers to gentle slopes covered with vegetation	Soft sandstone & siltstone	None documented	None documented	Unknown	None documented	Potential scarring by off-road vehicles	None
	Sundance Fm.: Hulett Sandstone Member (Jsh)	Yellowish-brown very fine-grained glauconitic calcareous sandstone. Gradational lower & upper contacts. Sandstone in lower 1.5-3 m (5-10 ft) in beds less than 2.54 cm-.06 m (1 in-2 ft) thick separated by shale partings less than 2.54 cm-15 cm (1-6 in) thick; ripple marks. Middle part of mbr has massive sandstone beds 1.5-6 m (5-20 ft) thick. Upper 1.5-3 m (5-10 ft) is thin bedded, locally shale, & poorly cemented. Thickness averages 24 m (80 ft), range 18-27 m (60-90 ft).	Forms massive near-vertical, well-cemented cliff	High; resistant to weathering	None documented	None documented	Unknown	Rockfall & landslide potential	Prominent jointing may cause problems	Cliff nearly encircles Devils Tower
	Sundance Fm.: Stockade Beaver Shale Member (Jsb)	Thin sandstone at base contains black or dark-gray water-worn chert pebbles with a maximum dimension of about 5 cm (2 in). Above basal sand, lower half of mbr is mostly gray-green shale. Upper half is dark-gray to gray-green shale with interbedded fine-grained calcareous sandstone ranging from less than 0.3-1.8 m (1-6 ft) thick. Unconformable lower contact; gradational upper contact. No apparent fractures or joints. Thin-bedded; a few ripple marks. Thickness averages 21 m (70 ft), range 18-24 m (60-80 ft).	Poor to fair exposures; forms slopes	Low	None documented	None documented	Unknown	None documented	Easily scarred by off-road vehicles; erosion potential from development	None
	Sundance & Gypsum Spring Formations, undifferentiated (Jsg)	(see individual units)								
		Regional (J-2) Unconformity								
MIDDLE JURASSIC	Gypsum Spring Formation (Jgs)	White massive gypsum interbedded with red gypsiferous claystone & a few beds of gray cherty limestone & dolomite near top of formation. Laminated to thin bedded. Unconformable lower contact. Thickness averages 5-11 m (15 to 35 ft).	Good exposures; forms bare slopes	Low	None documented	Gypsum	Unknown	Gypsum karst outside monument; minor slumps & slides	Local joints in cherty limstone & dolomite, gypsum karst, & bare slopes may present problems	Thick gypsum beds; caps some oil reservoirs in Wyoming
		Regional (J-1) Unconformity								
PERMIAN TRIASSIC	Spearfish Formation[*] (TRPs)	Red clayey siltstone, siltstone, & sandstone with red sandy shale; beds of massive white gypsum in lower half; lower part not exposed. Poorly cemented. Thin to thick-bedded. Some joints in sandstone beds. Base not exposed. Uppermost 30 m (100 ft) exposed in Devils Tower NM.	Good exposures; forms bare slopes or conspicuous brownish-red to maroon cliffs	Low; weathers very easily	None found in Devils Tower but fossils of Triassic land vertebrates found in Wyoming	Gypsum	Unknown	None documented	Poorly cemented; Potential scarring from development	Massive gypsum Locally but not in monument

Robinson, Charles S. 1956. *Geology of Devils Tower National Monument, Wyoming.* Bulletin 1021-I. Denver, CO: U.S. Geological Survey.
[*] Robinson considered the Spearfish Formation to be a Triassic unit. Since 1956, the Spearfish Formation has been found to extend into the Permian.

Geologic History

This section describes the rocks and unconsolidated deposits that appear on the digital geologic map of Devils Tower National Monument, the environments in which those units were deposited, and the timing of geologic events that created the present landscape.

This section provides a more detailed description of the structure, tectonics, depositional and erosional history, and general stratigraphy of Devils Tower National Monument and the surrounding area. The Devils Tower and Black Hills region records a long and complex geologic history. At one time, Precambrian sediments that now compose the core of the Black Hills were buried about 14 km (9 mi) beneath the surface by Paleozoic, Mesozoic, and Cenozoic sediments. Intense heat and pressure at depth metamorphosed the Precambrian sediments and magma engulfed and injected itself into the rock. The metamorphosed and igneous rock units were uplifted during the Laramide Orogeny and erosion then exposed today's oval-shaped Black Hills (fig. 6). Cored by Precambrian rocks, the Black Hills are rimmed by Paleozoic and Mesozoic sedimentary strata. Devils Tower National Monument lies within the Black Hills region and is an erosional remnant of igneous activity generated during the Laramide Orogeny.

Precambrian History of the Black Hills Region

The Precambrian rocks exposed in the Black Hills are predominantly Early Proterozoic metasedimentary units (sedimentary rocks that have undergone metamorphism) that were deposited about 1,600–2,500 million years ago (Ma) (fig. 11). Understanding both the depositional and tectonic evolution of the Black Hills during the Precambrian is limited due to the complex geology and lack of precise age control for the metasedimentary rocks of the Black Hills. While age dates are available for igneous rocks in the Black Hills, precise ages for the metasedimentary rocks are lacking.

Correlations with units in surrounding areas are hampered by the fact that the Black Hills are more than 300 km (190 mi) from Precambrian outcrops in southern Wyoming and more than 1,100 km (680 mi) away from similar age rocks in Manitoba and Saskatchewan. Stratigraphic, depositional, tectonic, and chronologic studies on the Black Hills have resulted in the following general interpretations (Redden et al. 1990).

The Black Hills are underlain by Archean basement rocks about 2,500 million years old that belong to the Wyoming Archean Province (fig. 12). At the time these rocks were emplaced, Wyoming formed the southern margin of the landmass that would form the core of the North American craton. Prior to 2,170 Ma, an extensional (pull-apart) tectonic setting developed along the passive tectonic margin of the Wyoming Archean Province. Coarse-grained clastic rocks with local anomalous concentrations of uranium and minor

chromite were deposited from west-to-east in alluvial fans forming on continental Archean basement.

Between 1,980 Ma and 2,170 Ma, the extensional tectonic setting along the plate margin changed to one of compression (fig. 13). Gabbro sills (a type of intrusive igneous rock) intruded the Early Proterozoic strata and Archean basement about 2,170 Ma. Deformation caused folding about north-northwest trending axes. The deformation may record early activity in the development of the collision zone between the Wyoming Archean Province and the Trans-Hudson Province. Alluvial fans of quartz-rich, feldspathic sediment derived from the east bordered tidal flat and marine shelf environments to the west and south.

Black shale was deposited in a deepening basin in the Black Hills region about 2,000 Ma. This deposition was accompanied by the submarine eruption of basalt. Deep-water deposition by density currents (turbidites) flowing over the continental shelf and down the continental slope then followed. While a marine basin formed in the Black Hills region, the eastern margin of the Wyoming Archean Province, which was located east of the current Black Hills, was undergoing uplift, volcanism, and possibly deformation. Water depths increased from east to west and north to south.

A 90-million year time gap separates the turbidite deposits and basalt flows of the basin from overlying conglomerates, debris flows, and minor volcanic rocks. In some areas, the older rocks were folded and overturned by a deformational event that occurred prior to deposition of the younger sediments. The deformation is poorly understood, but the general northerly trend of the folds suggests another episode of east-west tectonic closure. Although speculative, the deformation may be attributed to plate margin effects along the Trans-Hudson and Wyoming Archean Province boundary.

A thick, widespread shale unit exposed in the central Black Hills was deposited between 1,710 and 1,880 Ma. The general lack of shallow-water structures suggests that the main basin in the current Black Hills region continued to evolve as an intracontinental or back-arc basin (fig. 13) from about 1,900–1,800 Ma.

All the stratified rocks and the Archean basement were folded along east-northeast axes sometime between about 1,710 and 1,850 Ma. After this folding event, but before 1,710 Ma, the stratified rocks and Archean basement were again folded along north-northwest axes and regionally metamorphosed. Rb-Sr age dates suggest that the metamorphism may have occurred about 1,840

Ma. The compressional events probably were associated with convergence of the Wyoming Archean Province with the Trans-Hudson Province.

The Harney Peak Granite, into which Mount Rushmore was carved, probably formed by melting of Archean crust and minor amounts of Early Proterozoic rocks about 1,710 Ma. Too young to be related to the Trans-Hudson deformation event that took place about 1,840–1,910 Ma, the Harney Peak Granite may be related to tectonic activity in the Central Plains Province to the south (fig. 12).

Paleozoic History of the Black Hills Region

Although only 6% of Earth's history is recorded in the Paleozoic Era (251–542 Ma) compared to the roughly 88% of Earth history represented by the Precambrian (542–4,600 Ma), the Paleozoic is comparatively rich in detail because of fossils. The Paleozoic strata that rim the core of the Black Hills, and the fossils they contain, record several episodes of marine deposition followed by subaerial erosion.

Cambrian and Ordovician sandstone, glauconitic shale, limestone, and dolomite were deposited in marine environments although the shoreline did not reach Wyoming until Middle Cambrian time (Boyd 1993; Driscoll et al. 2002). Sea level rose in the latest Cambrian and flooded almost the entire North American continent, leaving a strip of land or a series of islands exposed along what is known as the Transcontinental Arch, an upland that stretched from northern Minnesota southwestward across South Dakota, northwestern Nebraska, Colorado and northwestern New Mexico (fig. 14). Before the end of the Early Ordovician, the sea regressed off the craton and erosion stripped much of the Cambrian and Ordovician strata from the area during the Devonian. Silurian age rocks are not present in the Black Hills. They may have been eroded during the Devonian or were never deposited.

During Middle Devonian to Middle Mississippian time, the western margin of North America was undergoing compression as the North American lithospheric plate collided with the Pacific Plate, causing the Antler Orogeny (fig. 11). This collision caused a series of Devonian transgressions during which the shoreline advanced from west to east onto the craton, depositing marine sediments throughout the northern and western part of Wyoming (Boyd 1993). In the Late Devonian to Early Mississippian, a major regression was followed by yet another west to east transgression (fig. 15).

In some cratonic basins such as the Williston Basin in North Dakota and Montana (fig. 14), the black marine shale of the Devonian Bakken Formation is a prolific petroleum source rock. In the Black Hills, the widespread Mississippian-age Madison, or Pahasapa, Limestone was deposited in a warm, shallow-water environment. When the sea regressed in the Late Mississippian, elaborate karst (solution) features developed in the Madison Limestone, including those seen at Wind Cave National Park and Jewel Cave National Monument in South Dakota. Today, the Madison Limestone is a major aquifer in the Black Hills region.

At the end of the Paleozoic, the major landmasses were coming together to form a supercontinent called Pangaea. Wyoming was located along the western margin of Pangaea. The South American landmass collided with the southern margin of North America, generating the forces responsible for the Ancestral Rockies in Colorado. In general, the Pennsylvanian and Permian strata in Wyoming record episodic transgressive and regressive cycles (Boyd 1993). Terrestrial redbeds are interlayered with marine carbonates, sandstone, and phosphatic and cherty strata.

By the end of Middle Permian time, the shoreline had shifted to the west and near-shore, shallow marine clastics of the lower Spearfish Formation were deposited in the Black Hills and Devils Tower region (Sabel 1981, 1984). Bedded gypsum, salt casts in rippled siltstone, and micritic limestone and dolomite suggest subaqueous, hypersaline environments of deposition for the lower Spearfish. Stromatolites and oscillation ripples indicate periods of shallow marine conditions. At the end of the Permian, this area was located approximately 30° north latitude. Today, a similar hot arid climate and depositional environment is found in the marginal marine sabkhas (salt flats) of the Persian Gulf region.

Mesozoic History of the Black Hills Region

Triassic Period

By the Early Triassic, the major landmasses had come together to form Pangaea (fig. 16). An Early Triassic sea flooded eastward and transgressed quickly over the gently westward sloping central Wyoming shelf (Picard 1993; Dubiel 1994). The Early Triassic part of the Spearfish Formation represents a low gradient, coastal plain environment located east of this advancing sea (Robinson 1956; Sabel 1981, 1984; Picard 1993). Intermittent fluvial systems developed along with isolated bodies of water. High evaporation rates encouraged the growth of algal mats. Dolomites, limestones, and sulfates precipitated in these bodies of water, which were recharged by runoff and saline groundwater.

Jurassic Period

By the end of the Triassic, Pangaea was breaking apart and the landmasses began migrating to their current positions. A period of uplift and erosion occurred following the deposition of the Spearfish Formation. A shallow epicontinental seaway inundated large portions of the Western Interior of North America, a physiographic province bordered to the west by a rising mountain range caused by the Sevier Orogeny and to the east by the stable North American craton (Brenner 1983; Kvale et al. 2001). The Ancestral Rocky Mountains separated this seaway from the Gulf of Mexico, and in some areas, the seaway may have been less than 500 km (300 mi) wide.

Tectonism caused global eustatic sea level fluctuations so that this shallow seaway spread southward from the

Arctic to inundate the Western Interior in a series of transgressive-regressive sequences that are stratigraphically packaged between unconformities (Pipiringos and O'Sullivan 1978; Brenner and Peterson 1994; Peterson 1994; Kvale et al. 2001). At this time, Wyoming lay within 15°–20° North latitude, and the abundance of red beds, evaporites, and shallow water carbonates suggest that Jurassic paleoclimate in the Devils Tower National Monument region was generally warm and dry (Saleeby and Busby-Spera 1992; Kvale et al. 2001).

In the Early Jurassic, the inland sea transgressed from the north to inundate western Montana and the Williston Basin area of Montana and North Dakota (Brenner and Peterson 1994; Peterson 1994). Vast ergs (eolian sand seas) developed south of the epicontinental seaway in Utah, Colorado, New Mexico, and Arizona. Early Jurassic deposits are not represented in the Devils Tower region.

The Middle Jurassic Gypsum Spring Formation represents a return of the sea into the area following an Early Jurassic shoreline regression and records the first of two Middle Jurassic transgressive-regressive depositional cycles (Brenner and Peterson 1994; Peterson 1994; Kvale et al. 2001). The depocenter of the Middle Jurassic inland sea was located in central Utah and westernmost Wyoming (fig. 17). East of the depocenter, the average depth of the shallow sea was less than 100 m (300 ft).

Thicker in western Wyoming, the Gypsum Spring Formation thins to the east and southeast (Picard 1993). In central Wyoming and the Big Horn Basin in north-central Wyoming, the Gypsum Spring Formation has been divided into a lower unit consisting of interbedded evaporites and siltstones deposited in a sabkha type environment that was periodically flooded; a middle unit of interbedded limestones and dolomites that were deposited in a shallow, warm water subtidal environment; and an upper unit of nodular and interbedded evaporites and siltstones deposited in another sabkha type environment (Picard 1993, 1997; Guyer 2000). The thick gypsum and anhydrite masses of the lower unit are predominantly microcrystalline (Williams and Parcell 2003). The middle unit contains several species of ammonites, pelecypods, and crinoids.

Extensive reefs developed in many parts of the globe during the Jurassic and Middle Jurassic. Microbial buildups have been recognized in the Gypsum Spring Formation in the Big Horn Basin. These reefs record some of the earliest known occurrence of Jurassic microbial reefs in North America (Parcell and Williams 2003; Ploynoi and Parcell 2005). The buildups are composed of blue-green algae (cyanobacteria), coralline red algae, green algae, encrusting foraminifera, encrusting bryozoa, sponges, corals, and mollusks. The buildups probably developed in shallow, possibly brackish water less than 1 m (3 ft) deep.

The contact between the Gypsum Spring Formation and underlying strata is one of the most prominent

unconformities in the Paleozoic and Mesozoic record of Montana, Wyoming, and Utah (Picard 1993; Peterson 1994; Schmude 1999). Today, the Gypsum Spring evaporites serve as caprocks (top seals) over Nugget Sandstone petroleum reservoirs in Wyoming and Utah (Picard 1993).

The shale, glauconitic sandstone, and limestone sequences of the Sundance Formation in the Black Hills record at least two transgressive-regressive cycles, including the last and most extensive transgression of the Jurassic age, which covered much of the Western Interior (Brenner 1983; Picard 1993; Kvale et al. 2001). The Stockade Beaver Shale, Hulett Sandstone, and Lak Members comprise the lower Sundance Formation and record a Middle Jurassic transgressive-regressive depositional cycle (Brenner and Peterson 1994; Peterson 1994). The marine Stockade Beaver Shale Member is overlain by the regressive marine Hulett Sandstone Member deposited in a variety of subenvironments of a barrier-island complex including shoreface and beach, tidal channels, and back-barrier lagoon and tidal flats (Picard 1993; Brenner and Peterson 1994). The lower Sundance Formation is capped by the red siltstones of the nonmarine Lak Member.

In eastern Wyoming, the upper Sundance Formation is represented by the greenish-gray shales and fossiliferous sandy limestones of the Redwater Shale Member, an Upper Jurassic transgressive-regressive depositional cycle (Brenner and Peterson 1994; Peterson 1994). While previous Jurassic regressions resulted from eustatic (worldwide) sea level falls, regression of the shoreline at the top of the Redwater Shale cycle was the result of an increase in siliciclastic sediment supply. Erosion of uplifting highlands to the west, generated by increased tectonic activity (Sevier Orogeny) along the North American west coast, accelerated sedimentation rates and filled the Western Interior Basin faster than the basin could respond to the Upper Jurassic eustatic rise in sea level (Hallam 1988; Brenner and Peterson 1994; Peterson 1994).

In the Bighorn Basin, rare Middle Jurassic dinosaur megatrack sites have been discovered in the Gypsum Spring Formation and the lower Sundance Formation (Kvale et al. 2001). Footprints in both formations are preserved in intertidal to supratidal coastal environments that were once thought to be marine in origin. Possible swim tracks in the Gypsum Spring Formation also have been assigned to bipedal dinosaurs and crocodilians (Kvale et al. 2001; Mickelson et al. 2005).

The Morrison Formation represents continental environments of deposition during the final retreat of the Jurassic seas. The Morrison Formation is a widespread nonmarine complex that covers most of the Western Interior. Lying on a scoured and channeled upper Sundance Formation, the Morrison attests to a change to terrestrial conditions. Alluvial fans, lakes, and braided and meandering streams are common environments in the Morrison (Picard 1993). The Morrison Formation is world renown for its dinosaur fossils and also contains significant uranium in fluvial sandstone deposits.

Cretaceous Period

Although the subduction zone was far to the west of the Black Hills region during the Sevier Orogeny, compressive forces caused by the collision were felt far inland. Cretaceous sedimentary rocks record deposition in a Western Interior foreland basin that formed, in part, as a flexural response to crustal loading by the fold-and-thrust belt of western North America and, in part, as a response to subduction of the Farallon plate (Dickinson 1974; Dickinson and Snyder 1978; Steidtmann 1993).

As the mountains rose in the west and the roughly north-south Western Interior Basin subsided, the Gulf of Mexico separating North and South America continued to rift open in the south, and marine water began to spill into the basin. At the same time, marine water began to transgress from the Arctic region in the north. Relative sea level rose and fell frequently throughout the Cretaceous so that Cretaceous sediments record a complex history of transgressive-regressive cycles.

The Lower Cretaceous sandstones, shales, minor carbonates and coal of the Lakota and Fall River Formations represent fluvial, floodplain, and marsh depositional environments. The Skull Creek Shale, Newcastle Sandstone, Mowry Shale, and Belle Fourche Shale in the Black Hills region record episodic fluctuations of relative sea level and were deposited in near-shore to off-shore depositional environments as the seaway expanded.

Eventually, the Upper Cretaceous seaway became the most extensive interior seaway ever to cover the continent (fig. 18). The Western Interior Seaway extended from today's Gulf of Mexico to the Arctic Ocean, a distance of about 4,827 km (3,000 mi) (Kauffman 1977; Steidtmann 1993). During periods of maximum transgression, the width of the basin was 1,600 km (1,000 mi). The basin was relatively unrestricted at either terminus.

At the close of the Cretaceous, the Western Interior Seaway drained from the area of the future Black Hills uplift. The seas gradually receded, and a shallowing-upward sequence of sedimentation developed from the offshore marine Pierre Shale to the near-shore marine Fox Hills Sandstone (exposed in Wyoming and the Dakotas but not in the Black Hills) and the fluvio-deltaic Lance Formation/Hell Creek Formation (exposed in Wyoming and the Dakotas but not in the Black Hills). The Lance and equivalent Hells Creek formations were deposited within the last 3 million years of the Cretaceous (Driscoll et al. 2002). Streams flowed eastward from the east side of the Powder River Basin located in northeastern Wyoming, west of the present Black Hills region. These drainage patterns indicate that the Black Hills uplift did not yet exist.

Cenozoic History of the Black Hills Region

The Laramide Orogeny and Devils Tower

During the Late Cretaceous to Early Tertiary (75–35 Ma) Laramide Orogeny, thrust faults cut deeply into Earth's crust, thrusting ancient plutonic and metamorphic basement rocks to the surface and forming the modern Rocky Mountains. These thrust faults have steeply dipping fault planes at the surface that curve and become nearly horizontal at depth. Eventually, they reach Precambrian basement crystalline rock at depths up to 9 km (30,000 ft or 5.7 mi) below sea level (Gries, 1983; Erslev, 1993). In the Black Hills, ancient Precambrian margins involving the Wyoming Archean province and the Trans-Hudson province may have provided planes of weakness that influenced Laramide folding, faulting, and magmatic activity (Lisenbee and DeWitt 1993).

The basement-cored arches of the Rocky Mountains are bounded by thrust faults and separated by sediment-filled basins. The north-south trending, doubly-plunging Black Hills anticline is the easternmost expression of the Laramide Orogeny. The initial phase of uplift occurred in the Paleocene. With uplift, sediments were shed into the Powder River Basin and the Williston Basin to the north (fig. 19).

Two large blocks of Precambrian basement were thrust upward in the Black Hills region during the Laramide Orogeny (Karner and Halvorson 1989). Just west of the Missouri Buttes lies the Black Hills monocline that forms the western edge of the northern block. This northern block may have produced deep fractures in the crust that provided a route for magma to reach the surface. Several domes in this area formed from the vertical movement of magma prior to the emplacement of the Missouri Buttes and Devils Tower. Stocks, dikes, sills, and laccoliths were emplaced across the northern Black Hills uplift during this initial tectonism (62 Ma) (Lisenbee and DeWitt 1993). Near the end of the Eocene, magma approached or perhaps reached the surface. Devils Tower and Missouri Buttes were emplaced about 40 Ma and 50 Ma, respectively (Karner and Halvorson 1989). Both Devils Tower and Missouri Buttes lie within a depression formed within relatively horizontal sedimentary strata.

With Laramide uplift, deposition ceased and erosion began. Most of the present surface was exposed by late Oligocene time (Karner and Halvorson 1989). An estimated 200–1,000 m (660–3,300 ft) of sedimentary cover was eroded from Devils Tower.

Devils Tower

Detailed petrology of the Devils Tower phonolite porphyry shows phenocrysts of anorthoclase, aegirine-augite, and sphene in a trachytic groundmass consisting of the minerals albite, microcline, analcime, aegirine, nepheline, and nosean. Calcite, zeolites, hematite, clay, and analcime are common alteration or replacement products (Robinson 1956; Karner and Halvorson 1987, 1989). Green aegirine-augite is the principal mafic mineral and is found as phenocrysts and as groundmass needles. Analcime is one of the primary groundmass constituents.

As discussed previously in the "Geologic Features and Processes" section, four general hypotheses have been proposed for the origin of Devils Tower.

1. Devils Tower is an erosional remnant of a volcanic neck. In this hypothesis, the volcano vented to the

surface through more than a hundred meters (several hundred ft) of sediments (Carpenter 1988; Dutton and Schwartz 1936; Halvorson 1980; Karner and Halvorson 1987, 1989).

2. Devils Tower is a remnant of a laccoltih or sill (Jagger 1901; Darton 1901).

3. Devils Tower is an intrusive igneous body, such as a small pluton (Robinson 1956).

4. Devils Tower lies in a depression that is the remnant of a crater formed during an explosive volcanic episode when rising magma encountered meteoric groundwater. Devils Tower is the erosional remnant of the lava and hot pyroclastic material that filled this crater (Kiver and Harris 1999).

The nearly vertical columns in the center of Devils Tower and the outward flaring columns elsewhere around the base could have formed as part of a volcanic neck, shallow intrusion, or a sloping basin surface. Still, as explained in the aforementioned section, apparent discrepancies exist for all of the origin hypotheses.

Post-Laramide History of the Black Hills Region

A second phase of tectonic activity impacted the region in the latest Paleocene and Eocene, but by Late Eocene, the Laramide Orogeny was over and continental deposits of the White River Group covered the uplift. However, Eocene deposits fill paleo-valleys carved into the underlying strata, suggesting that the topographic form of the present Black Hills existed prior to deposition of these overlying sediments.

Widespread deposition, normal faulting, regional uplift, climatic changes, development of modern drainage systems, and basin excavation all occurred during the Neogene (Miocene and younger) in Wyoming (Flanagan and Montagne 1993). Abundant volcaniclastic detritus of remote origin and locally derived detrital sediments filled the Laramide basins during the Oligocene and Miocene. Many basins may have contained over 915 m (3,000 ft) of Miocene and Pliocene rocks (Flanagan and Montagne 1993). Erosion of the basins occurred after the establishment of large, through-flowing rivers in the Pliocene and Pleistocene.

Extensional (pull-apart) tectonics impacted northwest Wyoming around 17 Ma and 13 Ma (Flanagan and Montagne 1993). Normal faults, coupled with younger faults to the east and north and the mid-Miocene change in sedimentation in Nebraska, suggests that the faulting in Wyoming was related to the tectonism affecting the Basin and Range, Rio Grande Rift, and Snake River Plain at this time.

Regional uplift in the Black Hills and Devils Tower area occurred in a series of pulses. The first pulse occurred during the Laramide Orogeny. A second pulse occurred in the late Oligocene to early Miocene and caused a change in flow direction of some Rocky Mountain river systems and influenced conglomeratic sedimentation in Wyoming and Nebraska. The third and major pulse of uplift began in the mid-Miocene (about 17 Ma) and continued through the Pleistocene (Steidtmann et al. 1989; Flanagan and Montagne 1993; Mears, Jr. 1993). This last pulse is roughly contemporaneous with a period of volcanism in the Basin and Range province and in northwestern Wyoming. Wyoming was elevated to almost its present elevation during the mid-Miocene.

Recent erosion caused by the Belle Fourche River and its tributaries has exposed the current topographic expression of the tower. The alluvium, glacial materials, and other surficial deposits of Quaternary age fill major drainages in the area and continue to be deposited in a continental environment.

Eon	Era	Period	Epoch	Ma	Life Forms	N. American Tectonics
Phanerozoic (Phaneros = "evident"; zoic = "life")	Cenozoic	Quaternary	Holocene	0.01	Modern humans	Cascade volcanoes (W)
			Pleistocene		Extinction of large mammals and birds	Worldwide glaciation
				1.8		
		Tertiary	Pliocene		Large carnivores	Uplift of Sierra Nevada (W)
				5.3	Whales and apes	Linking of N. and S. America
			Miocene	23.0		
			Oligocene	33.9		Basin-and-Range extension (W)
			Eocene	55.8		
			Paleocene		Early primates	Laramide Orogeny ends (W)
				65.5		
	Mesozoic	Cretaceous			Mass extinction	Laramide Orogeny (W)
					Placental mammals	Sevier Orogeny (W)
				145.5	Early flowering plants	Nevadan Orogeny (W)
		Jurassic			First mammals	Elko Orogeny (W)
				199.6	Mass extinction	Breakup of Pangaea begins
		Triassic			Flying reptiles	Sonoma Orogeny (W)
					First dinosaurs	
				251		
	Paleozoic	Permian			Mass extinction	Supercontinent Pangaea intact
					Coal-forming forests diminish	Ouachita Orogeny (S)
						Alleghenian (Appalachian) Orogeny (E)
				299		Ancestral Rocky Mts. (W)
		Pennsylvanian			Coal-forming swamps	
					Sharks abundant	
				318.1	Variety of insects	
		Mississippian			First amphibians	
				359.2	First reptiles	Antler Orogeny (W)
		Devonian			Mass extinction	
					First forests (evergreens)	Acadian Orogeny (E-NE)
				416		
		Silurian			First land plants	
				443.7	Mass extinction	
		Ordovician			First primitive fish	
					Trilobite maximum	Taconic Orogeny (NE)
					Rise of corals	
				488.3		
		Cambrian				Avalonian Orogeny (NE)
					Early shelled organisms	Extensive oceans cover most of N. America
				542		
Proterozoic ("Early life")		Precambrian			First multicelled organisms	Formation of early supercontinent Grenville Orogeny (E)
						First iron deposits
					Jellyfish fossil (670 Ma)	Abundant carbonate rocks
				2500		
Archean ("Ancient")					Early bacteria and algae	
				~4000		Oldest known Earth rocks (~3.96 billion years ago)
Hadean ("Beneath the Earth")					Origin of life?	Oldest moon rocks (4-4.6 billion years ago)
						Earth's crust being formed
				4600	Formation of the Earth	

Life Forms side labels: Age of Mammals; Age of Dinosaurs; Age of Amphibians; Fishes; Marine Invertebrates.

Figure 11. Generalized geologic time scale; adapted from the U.S. Geological Survey and International Commission on Stratigraphy. Red lines indicate major unconformities between eras. Included are major events in life history and tectonic events occurring on the North American continent. Absolute ages shown are in millions of years (Ma). Events specific to Devils Tower National Monument are discussed in the text.

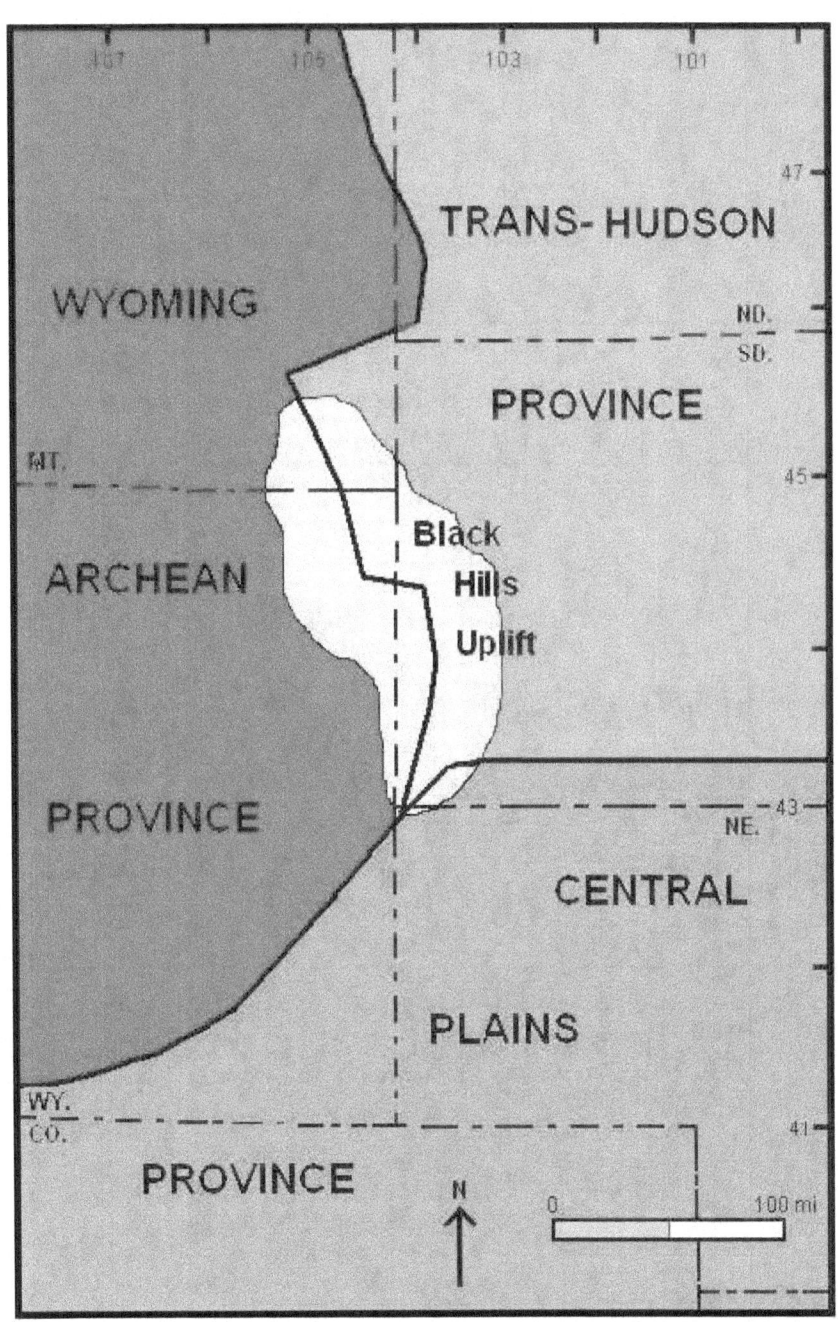

Figure 12. Location of the current Black Hills Uplift with regards to Precambrian terranes, northern Great Plains region. Modified from Lisenbee and DeWitt (1993).

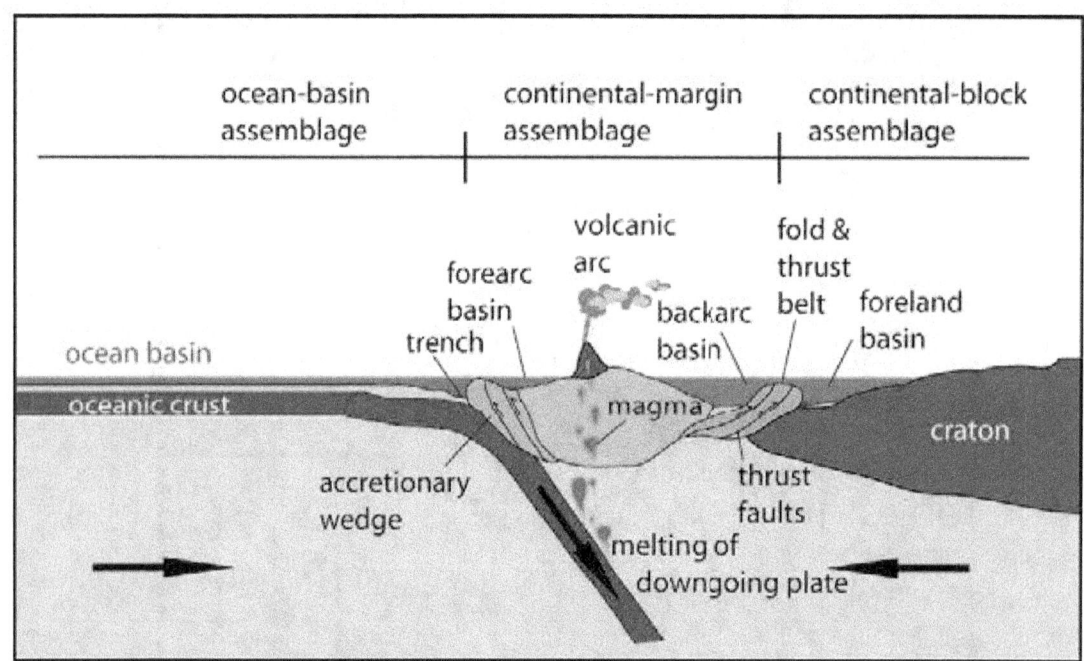

Figure 13. Plate tectonic schematic illustrating some of the Precambrian tectonic activity in the Black Hills region. In this drawing, the subducting lithosphere would represent the Trans-Hudson Province being subducted beneath the Wyoming Archean Province. The Black Hills and Devils Tower National Monument region would be located in the area of the Back-arc basin between 1,710 and 1,880 Ma. A similar tectonic setting exists today off the coast of China and Japan in the western Pacific Ocean. Graphic by Trista Thornberry-Ehrlich.

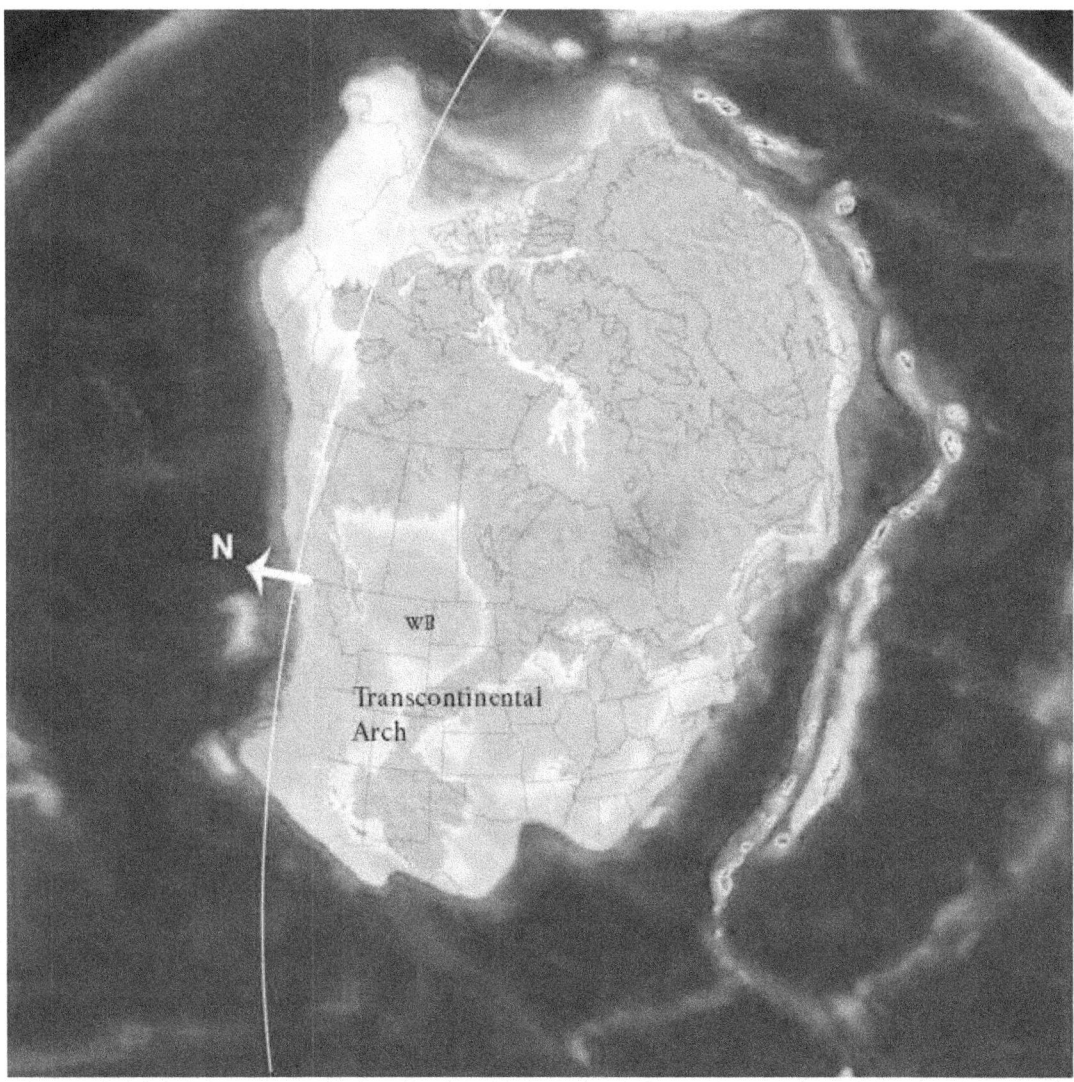

Figure 14. Paleogeographic map of the Late Cambrian, about 500 Ma. The Transcontinental Arch is the narrow landmass that transects South Dakota, northwestern Nebraska, and Colorado. Relatively shallow water and nearshore environments occupy the region of the Black Hills while a deeper water basin (darker shade of blue) is forming in the area of the Williston Basin (WB). Modified from Dr. Ron Blakey, Northern Arizona University, http://jan.ucc.nau.edu/~rcb7/namC500.jpg (access February 27, 2006).

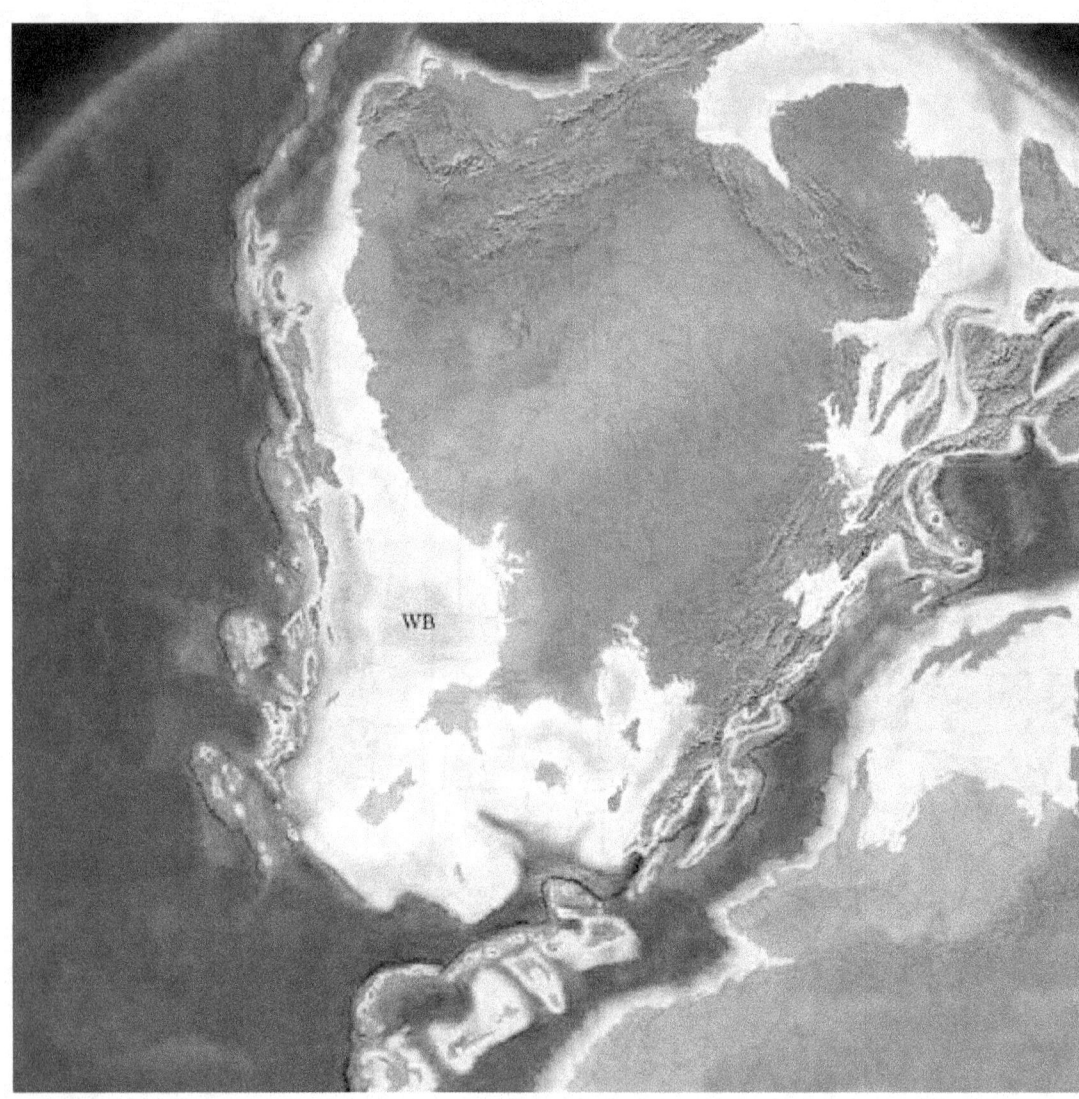

Figure 15. Paleogeographic map of North America during the Early Mississippian Period, about 345 Ma. Note that much of the conterminous United States is covered with a shallow sea, including the area of the Black Hills, and the Transcontinental Arch has been breached. The Williston Basin (WB) continues to be a physiographic feature at this time. Modified from Dr. Ron Blakey, Northern Arizona University, http://jan.ucc.nau.edu/~rcb7/namM345.jpg (access February 27, 2006).

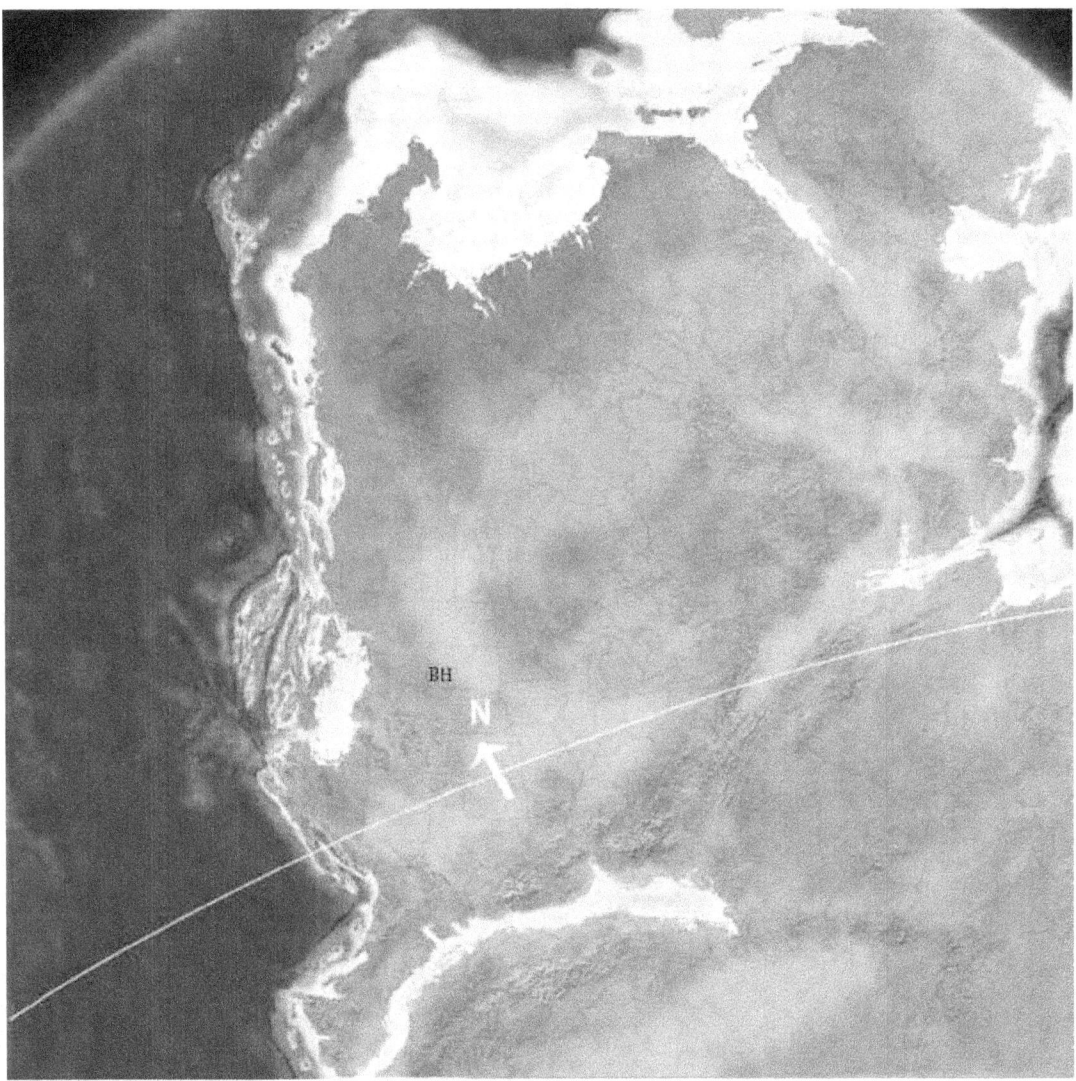

Figure 16. Paleogeographic map of North America during the Early Triassic Period, about 245 Ma, during deposition of the upper Spearfish Formation. The landmasses had come together at this time to form the supercontinent, Pangaea. Inland and near the Equator, eastern Wyoming's climate was hot and arid. The eventual Black Hills (BH) region was surrounded by lowlands containing redbeds and sabkha-like environments. Remnants of the Ancestral Rocky Mountains can still be seen in Colorado. Modified from Dr. Ron Blakey, Northern Arizona University, http://jan.ucc.nau.edu/~rcb7/namTr245.jpg (access February 27, 2006).

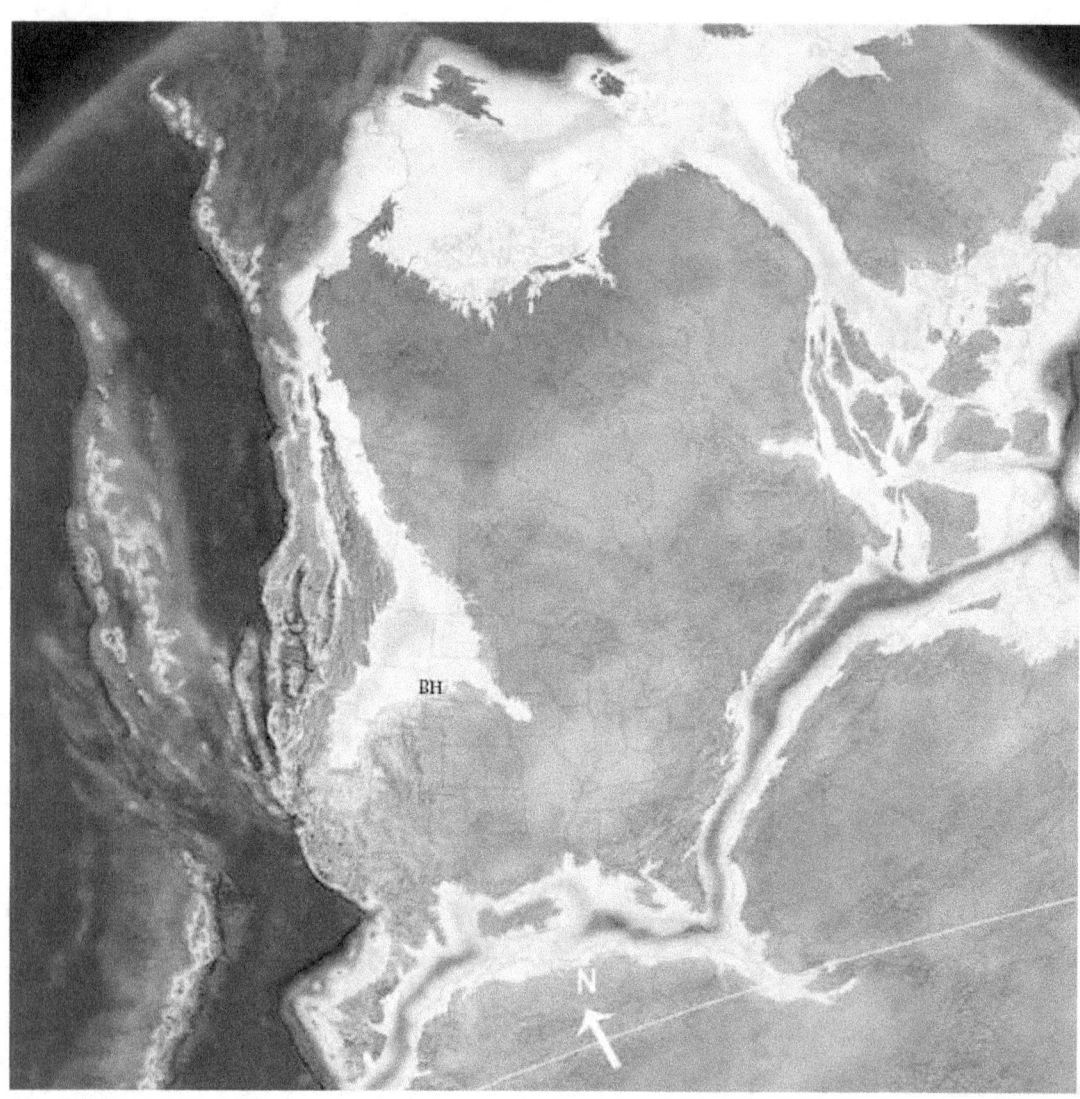

Figure 17. Paleogeographic map of North America during the Jurassic Period, about 170 Ma. The Western Interior of North America has been inundated by shallow marine environments. BH: eventual Black Hills region. Modified from Dr. Ron Blakey, Northern Arizona University, http://jan.ucc.nau.edu/~rcb7/namJ170.jpg (access February 27, 2006).

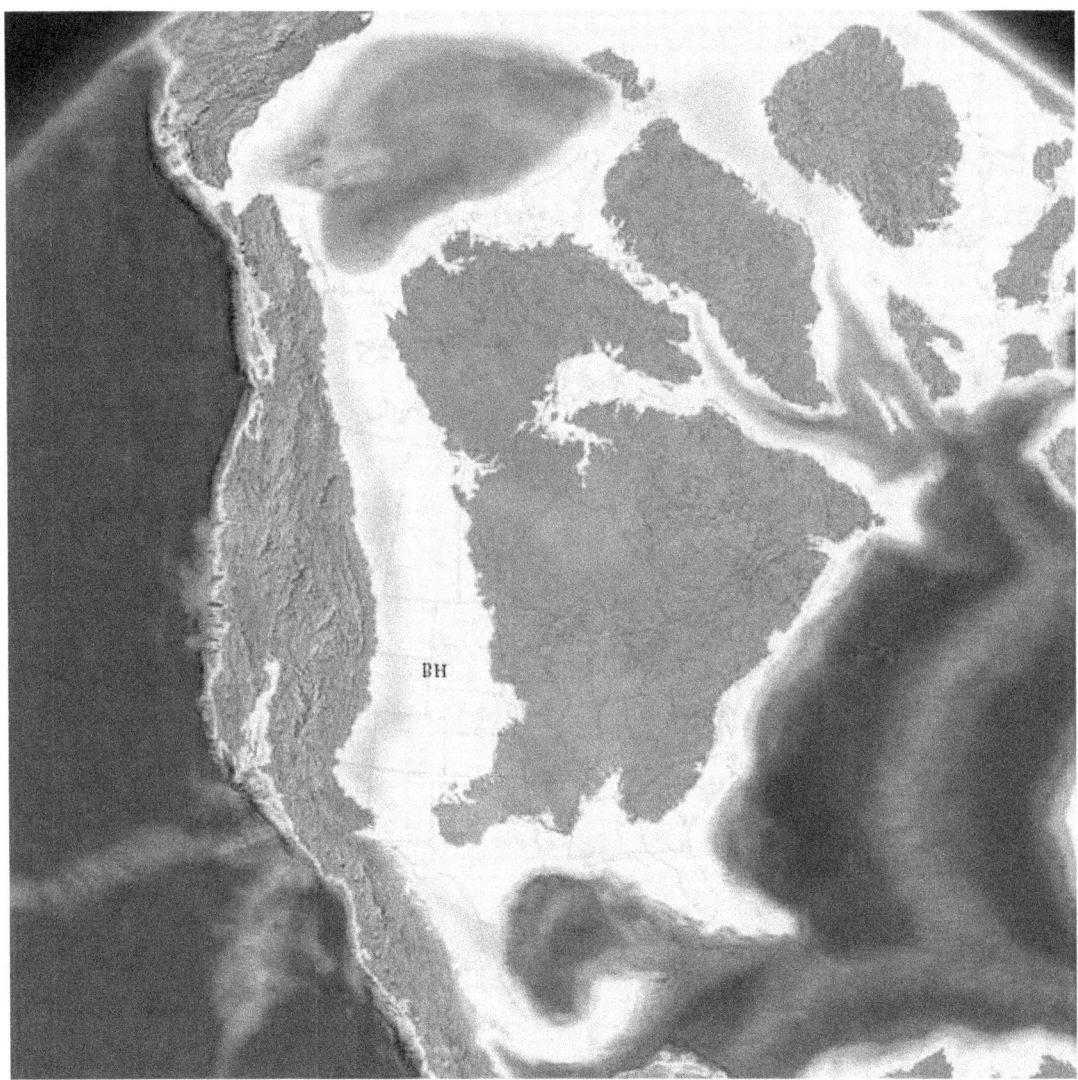

Figure 18. Western Interior Seaway during the Cretaceous, about 85 million years ago. Relatively shallow water covered the Devils Tower National Monument region at this time. BH: eventual Black Hills area. Modified from Dr. Ron Blakey, Northern Arizona University, http://jan.ucc.nau.edu/~rcb7/namK85.jpg (access February 27, 2006).

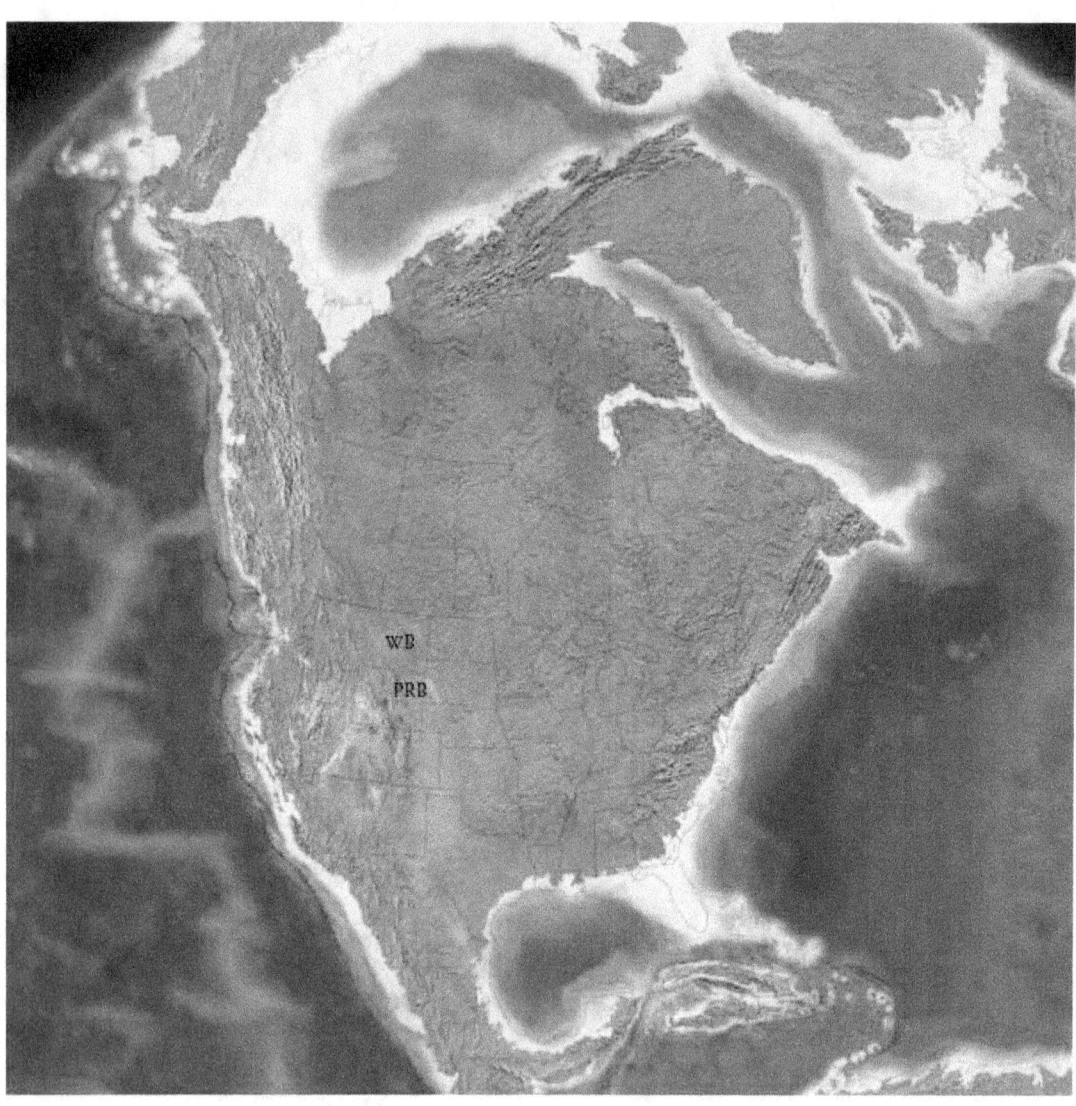

Figure 19. Paleogeography of the Black Hills region near the end of the Laramide Orogeny approximately 40 Ma. The Black Hills uplift is the easternmost expression of the Laramide Orogeny. PRB: Powder River Basin, which formed west of the Black Hills. WB: Williston Basin. Both basins are prolific hydrocarbon-producing basins. Modified from Dr. Ron Blakey, Northern Arizona University, http://jan.ucc.nau.edu/~rcb7/namPe40.jpg (access February 14, 2008).

Glossary

This glossary contains brief definitions of technical geologic terms used in this report. Not all geologic terms used are referenced. For more detailed definitions or to find terms not listed here please visit http://wrgis.wr.usgs.gov/docs/parks/misc/glossarya.html.

active tectonic margin. A continental margin at which there is significant seismicity and deformation caused by tectonic plate convergence.

alloclastic breccia. A breccia that is formed by disruption of nonvolcanic rocks by volcanic processes beneath Earth's surface; a type of volcanic breccia.

alluvial fan. A fan-shaped deposit of sediment that accumulates where a high gradient stream flows out of a mountain front into an area of lesser gradient such as a valley.

alluvium. Stream-deposited sediment that is generally rounded, sorted, and stratified.

aquifer. Rock or sediment that are sufficiently porous, permeable, and saturated to be useful as a source of water.

axis (fold). A straight line approximation that when moved parallel to itself generates the shape of a fold.

basement. The undifferentiated rocks, commonly igneous and metamorphic, that underlie the rocks of interest.

basin (structural). A doubly-plunging syncline in which rocks dip inward from all sides (also see dome).

basin (sedimentary). Any depression, from continental to local scales, into which sediments are deposited.

beach. A gently sloping shoreline covered with sediment, often formed by action of waves and tides.

bed. The smallest sedimentary strata unit, commonly ranging in thickness from one centimeter to a meter or two and distinguishable from beds above.

bedding. Depositional layering or stratification of sediments.

block (fault). A crustal unit bounded by faults, either completely or in part.

breccia. A coarse-grained, generally unsorted, sedimentary rock consisting of cemented angular clasts.

calcareous. A rock or sediment containing calcium carbonate.

carbonaceous. A rock or sediment with considerable carbon, esp. organics, hydrocarbons, or coal.

clastic. Rock or sediment made of fragments or pre-existing rocks.

clay. Clay minerals or sedimentary fragments the size of clay minerals (<2 cm).

cone-in-cone. A sedimentary structure that resembles a set of concentric cones fitting one into another in inverted positions (base upward, apex downward).

conglomerate. A coarse-grained sedimentary rock with clasts larger than 2 mm in a fine-grained matrix.

craton. The relatively old and geologically stable interior of a continent.

cross-stratification. Arrangement of strata inclined at an angle to the main, relatively horizontal layers of sedimentary rock.

crust. The outermost compositional shell of Earth, 10-40 km (6-25 mi) thick, consisting predominantly of relatively low-density silicate minerals.

crystalline. Describes the structure of a regular, orderly, repeating geometric arrangement of atoms

debris flow. A rapid and often sudden flow or slide of rock and soil material involving a wide range of types and sizes.

deformation. A general term for the process of faulting, folding, shearing, extension, or compression of rocks as a result of various Earth forces.

delta. A sediment wedge deposited at a stream's mouth where it flows into a lake or sea.

dike. A tabular igneous intrusion that cuts across or is at an angle to the orientation of adjacent rocks.

dip. The angle between a structural surface and a horizontal reference plane measured normal to their line of intersection.

dome. A doubly plunging anticline that dips radially in all directions.

eolian. Formed, eroded, or deposited by or related to the action of the wind.

eustatic. Relates to simultaneous worldwide rise or fall of sea level in Earth's oceans.

evaporite. Chemically precipitated mineral(s) formed by the evaporation of solute-rich water under restricted conditions.

extrusive. Of or pertaining to the eruption of igneous material onto the surface of Earth.

fault. A subplanar break in rock along which relative movement occurs between the two sides.

feldspar. A group of framework silicates, containing aluminum and calcium, sodium, or potassium; feldspars are the most abundant minerals in Earth's crust.

fissle. A property of splitting easily along closely spaced parallel planes.

foreland (tectonic). The exterior area of an orogenic belt where deformation occurs without significant metamorphism. Generally the foreland is closer to the continental interior than other portions of the orogenic belt.

foreland basin. A linear sedimentary basin in a foreland These basin subside in response to flexural loading of the lithosphere by thrust sheets.

formation. Fundamental rock-stratigraphic unit that is mappable and lithologically distinct from adjoining strata and has definable upper and lower contacts.

fracture. Irregular breakage of a mineral; also any break in a rock (e.g., crack, joint, fault)

igneous. Refers to a rock or mineral that originated from molten material; one of the three main classes or rocks: igneous, metamorphic, and sedimentary.

intrusion. A body of igneous rock that invades older rock. The invading rock may be a plastic solid or magma that pushes its way into the older rock.

joint. A semi-planar break in rock without relative movement of rocks on either side of the fracture surface.

karst topography. Topography characterized by abundant sinkholes and caverns formed by the dissolution of calcareous rocks.

laccolith. A tack head- to arcuate-shaped pluton that domed or up-arched the overlying country rocks and whose basal contact is parallel to the orientation of adjacent strata.

landslide. Any process or landform resulting from rapid mass movement under relatively dry conditions.

lava. Magma that has been extruded out onto Earth's surface, both molten and solidified.

lopolith. A large, typically layered igneous intrusion whose floor is concave and whose roof may be concave or flat.

lithosphere. The relatively rigid outmost shell of Earth's structure, 50 to 100 km (31 to 62 mi) thick, that encompasses the crust and uppermost mantle.

mafic. A rock, magma, or mineral rich in magnesium and iron.

magma. Molten rock generated within Earth that is the parent of igneous rocks.

mantle. The zone of Earth's interior between crust and core.

matrix. The fine-grained interstitial material between coarse grains in porphyritic igneous rocks and poorly sorted clastic sediments or rocks.

member. A lithostratigraphic unit with definable contacts that subdivides a formation.

metamorphic. Pertaining to the process of metamorphism or to its results.

metamorphism. Literally, "change in form". Metamorphism occurs in rocks with mineral alteration, genesis, and/or recrystallization from increased heat and pressure.

monocline. A one-limbed flexure in strata, which are usually flat-lying except in the flexure itself.

neck (volcanic). An eroded, semi-vertical, pipe-like discordant pluton that represents the vent of a volcano.

normal fault. A dip-slip fault in which the hanging wall moves down relative to the footwall.

orogeny. A mountain-building event, particularly a well-recognized event in the geological past (e.g. the Laramide Orogeny).

outcrop. Any part of a rock mass or formation that is exposed or "crops out" at Earth's surface.

paleogeography. The study, description, and reconstruction of the physical geography from past geologic periods.

Pangaea. A theoretical, single supercontinent that existed during the Permian and Triassic Periods (also see Laurasia and Gondwana).

passive tectonic margin. A continental boundary formed by rifting (pulling apart) and continental rupture and without plate-boundary tectonism.

pebble. Generally, small, rounded, rock particles from 4 to 64 mm in diameter.

phenocrysts. A coarse crystal in a *porphyritic* igneous rock.

phonolite. A group of fine-grained extrusive rocks primarily composed of feldspar minerals.

pluton. A body of intrusive igneous rock crystallized at some depth in Earth.

porphyry. An igneous rock with abundant coarse crystals in a fine-grained groundmass.

pyroxene. A group of dark rock-forming silicate minerals.

red beds. Sedimentary strata composed largely of sandstone, siltstone, and shale that are predominantly red due to the presence of ferric oxide (hematite) coating individual grains.

regression. A long-term seaward retreat of the shoreline or relative fall of sea level.

reverse fault. A contractional, high angle (>45°), dip-slip fault in which the hanging wall moves up relative to the footwall (also see thrust fault).

ripple marks. The undulating, subparallel, usually small-scale, ridge pattern formed on sediment by the flow of wind or water.

sabkha. A coastal environment in an arid climate where evaporation rates are high.

sandstone. Clastic sedimentary rock of predominantly sand-sized grains.

scarp. A steep cliff or topographic step resulting from vertical displacement on a fault or by mass movement.

sediment. An eroded and deposited, unconsolidated accumulation of lithic and mineral fragments.

sedimentary rock. A consolidated and lithified rock consisting of detrital and/or chemical sediment(s).

shale. A clastic sedimentary rock made of clay-sized particles that exhibit parallel splitting properties.

sill. A tabular, igneous intrusion that parallels the orientation of adjacent strata.

silt. Clastic sedimentary material intermediate in size between fine-grained sand and coarse clay (1/256-1/16 mm).

siltstone. A variable-lithified sedimentary rock with silt-sized grains.

stock. An igneous intrusion exposed less than 104 sq km (40 sq mi) at the surface.

strata. Tabular or sheetlike masses or distinct layers (e.g., of rock).

stratigraphy. The geologic study of the origin, occurrence, distribution, classification, correlation, age, etc. of rock layers, especially sedimentary rocks.

stream. Any body of water moving under gravity flow and confined within a channel.

subduction zone. A convergent plate boundary where oceanic lithosphere descends beneath a continental or oceanic plate and is carried down into the mantle.

subsidence. The gradual sinking or depression of part of Earth's surface.

talus. Rock fragments of any size or shape derived from and lying at the base of a cliff or very steep, rocky slope.

tectonic. Relating to large-scale movement and deformation of Earth's crust.

terrane. A region or group of rocks with similar geology, age, or structural style.

terrestrial. Relating to Earth or Earth's dry land.

thrust fault. A contractional, dip-slip fault with a shallowly dipping fault surface (<45°) where the hanging wall moves up and over relative to the footwall.

thrust sheet. The body of rock above a large-scale thrust fault whose surface is horizontal or very gently dipping.

topography. The general morphology of Earth's surface including relief and location of natural and anthropogenic features.

transgression. Landward migration of the sea due to a relative rise in sea level.

trend. The direction or azimuth of elongation or a linear geological feature.

turbidite. A sediment or rock deposited from, or inferred to have been deposited from, a turbidity (density) current.

unconformity. A surface within sedimentary strata that marks a prolonged period of nondeposition or erosion.

uplift. A structurally high area in the crust, produced by movement that raises the rocks.

vent. An opening at the surface of Earth where volcanic materials emerge.

volcanic. Related to volcanoes; describes igneous rock crystallized at or near Earth's surface (e.g., lava).

weathering. The set of physical, chemical, and biological processes by which rock is broken down in place.

References

This section lists references cited in this report. A more complete geologic bibliography is available from the National Park Service Geologic Resources Division.

Boyd, D. W. 1993. Paleozoic history of Wyoming. In *Geology of Wyoming*, ed. A. W. Snoke, J. R. Steidtmann, and S. M. Roberts, 164-187. Geological Survey of Wyoming, Memoir 5.

Brenner, R. L. 1983. Late Jurassic tectonic setting and paleogeography of Western Interior, North America. In *Mesozoic paleogeography of the west-central United States*, ed. M. W. Reynolds and E. D. Dolly, 119-133. Society of Economic Paleontologists and Mineralogists, Rocky Mountain Section, Rocky Mountain Paleogeography Symposium 2.

Brenner, R. L., and J. A. Peterson. 1994. Jurassic sedimentary history of the northern portion of the Western Interior Seaway, USA. In *Mesozoic systems of the Rocky Mountain region, USA*, ed. M. V. Caputo, J. A. Peterson, and K. J. Franczyk, 217-232. Society for Sedimentary Geology, Rocky Mountain Section.

Carpenter, F.R. 1888. *Notes on the ecology of the Black Hills. Rapid City*: Preliminary report of the South Dakota School of Mines.

Darton, N.H. 1909. Geology and water resources of the northern portion of the Black Hills and adjoining regions in South Dakota and Wyoming. Professional Paper 65. Denver, CO: U.S. Geological Survey.

Davis, A. D., and F. Beaver. 2002. Engineering problems of gypsum karst along the Interstate 90 development corridor in the Black Hills, South Dakota. *Geological Society of America Abstracts with Programs 34*: 216.

Dickinson, W. R. 1974. Plate tectonics and sedimentation. In *Tectonics and sedimentation*, ed. W. R. Dickinson, 1-27. Society of Economic Paleontologists and Mineralogists, Special Publication 22.

Dickinson, W. R., and W.S. Snyder. 1978. Plate tectonics of the Laramide Orogeny. In *Laramide folding associated with basement block faulting in the western United States*, ed. V. Matthews III, 355-366. Geological Society of America, Memoir 151.

Driscoll, D. G., J. M. Carter, J. E. Williamson, and L. D. Putman. 2002. *Hydrology of the Black Hills area, South Dakota*. U.S. Geological Survey, Water-Resources Investigations Report 02-4094. http://www.pubs.usgs.gov /wri/wri024094/pdf (accessed February 9, 2006).

Dubiel, R. F. 1994. Triassic deposystems, paleogeography, and paleoclimate of the Western Interior. In *Mesozoic Systems of the Rocky Mountain Region, USA*, ed. M. V. Caputo, J. A. Peterson, and K. J. Franczyk, 133-168. Society for Sedimentary Geology, Rocky Mountain Section.

Dutton, C.E., and G.M. Schwartz. 1936. Notes on the jointing of the Devil's Tower, Wyoming. *Journal of Geology* 44 (6): 717-728.

Effinger, W. L. 1934. *A report on the geology of Devils Tower National Monument.* National Park Service. http://www.cr.nps.gov/history/online_books/berkeley /effinger1/index.htm (accessed March 1, 2006).

Epstein, J. B. 2002. Gypsum-anhydrite karst in the Black Hills, South Dakota-Wyoming. *Geological Society of America Abstracts with Programs* 34: 116.

Epstein, J. B. 2003. Gypsum karst in the Black Hills, South Dakota-Wyoming: Geomorphic development, hazards, and hydrology. Circular. Norman: Oklahoma Geological Survey.

Erslev, E. A. 1993. Thrusts, back-thrusts, and detachment of Rocky Mountain foreland arches. In *Laramide basement deformation in the Rocky Mountain foreland of the western United States*, ed. C. J. Schmidt, R. B. Chase, and E. A. Erslev, 339-358. Geological Society of America, Special Paper 280.

Flanagan, K. M., and J. Montagne. 1993. Neogene stratigraphy and tectonics of Wyoming. In *Geology of Wyoming*, ed. A. W. Snoke, J. R. Steidtmann, and S. M. Roberts, 572-607. Geological Survey of Wyoming, Memoir 5.

Gries, R. 1983. North-south compression of Rocky Mountain foreland structures. In *Rocky Mountain foreland basins and uplifts*, ed. J. D. Lowell and R. Gries, 9-32. Rocky Mountain Association of Geologists.

Guyer, G. S. 2000. Paleoenvironments of the Jurassic Gypsum Spring Formation, Bighorn Basin, Wyoming. MS thesis, Iowa State University.

Hallam, A. 1988. A reevaluation of Jurassic eustasy in light of new data and the revised Exxon curve. In *Sea-Level changes - an integrated approach*, ed. C. K. Wilgus, B. S. Hastings, H. Posamentier, V. Wagoner, C. A. Ross, and C. G. Kendall, 261-273. Society of Economic Paleontologists and Mineralogists, Special Publication 42.

Halvorson, D. L. 1980. Geology and petrology of the Devils Tower, Missouri Buttes, and Barlow Canyon area, Crook County, Wyoming. PhD diss, University of North Dakota.

Harp, Edwin L., and Charles R. Lindsay. 2005. Stability of Leaning Column at Devils Tower National Monument, Wyoming. Denver: U.S. Geological Survey, Central Geologic Hazards Team. Report conveyed to Superintendent Lisa Eckert, Devils Tower National Monument, October 6, 2005.

Jaggar Jr., T. A. 1901. *Laccoliths of the Black Hills*. U.S. Geological Survey 21st Annual Report (3).

Karner, F. R., and D. L. Halvorson. 1987. The Devils Tower, Bear Lodge Mountains, Cenozoic igneous complex, northeastern Wyoming. In *Rocky Mountain Section of the Geological Society of America*, ed. S. S. Beus, 161-164. Geological Society of America, Centennial Field Guide 2.

Karner, F. R., and D. L. Halvorson. 1989. Devils Tower and the Missouri Buttes. In *Devils Tower – Black Hills alkalic igneous rocks and general geology*, ed. F. R. Karner, 67-69. Field Trip Guidebook T131. Washington, D.C.: American Geophysical Union.

Kauffman, E. G. 1977. Geological and biological overview: Western Interior Cretaceous basin. *Mountain Geologist* (14): 75-99.

Kiver, E. P., and D. V. Harris. 1999. Geology of U.S. parklands. 5th ed. New York: John Wiley & Sons, Inc.

Kvale, E. P., G. D. Johnson, D. L. Mickelson, K. Keller, L. C. Furer, and A. W. Archer. 2001. Middle Jurassic (Bajocian and Bathonian) dinosaur megatracksites, Bighorn Basin, Wyoming, U.S.A. *Palaios* (16): 233-254.

Lisenbee, A. L., and E. DeWitt. 1993. Laramide evolution of the Black Hills uplift. In *Geology of Wyoming*, ed. A. W. Snoke, J. R. Steidtmann, and S. M. Roberts, 374-412. Geological Survey of Wyoming, Memoir 5.

Mears, Jr., B. 1993. Geomorphic history of Wyoming and high-level erosion surfaces. In *Geology of Wyoming*, ed. A. W. Snoke, J. R. Steidtmann, and S. M. Roberts, 608-626. Geological Survey of Wyoming, Memoir 5.

Mickelson, D. L., E. P. Kvale, G. D. Johnson, M. R. King, K. A. Mickelson, and P. Getty. 2005. Subaqueous tetrapod swim tracks from the Middle Jurassic; Big Horn Basin, Wyoming, U.S.A. *Geological Society of America Abstracts with Programs* 37: 37.

Miller, E. L., M. M. Miller, C. H. Stevens, J. E. Wright, and R. Madrid. 1992. Late Paleozoic paleogeographic and tectonic evolution of the western U.S. cordillera. In *The Cordilleran Orogen: Conterminous U.S.*, ed. B. C. Burchfiel, P. W. Lipman, and M. L. Zoback, 57-106. Geological Society of America, The Geology of North America G-3.

National Park Service. 2001. Final general management plan/ environmental impact statement, Devils Tower National Monument. National Park Service. http://www.nps.gov/deto/gmp_final/pdf/final_gmp.pdf (accessed March 1, 2006).

Parcell, W. C., and M. K. Williams. 2003. Thrombolite buildups in the Middle Jurassic Piper and Gypsum Spring Formations, Bighorn Basin, Wyoming. *American Association of Petroleum Geologists Annual Meeting Expanded Abstracts* 12: 132.

Peterson, F. 1994. Sand dunes, sabkhas, streams, and shallow seas: Jurassic paleogeography in the southern part of the Western Interior Basin. In *Mesozoic Systems of the Rocky Mountain Region, USA*, ed. M. V. Caputo, J. A. Peterson, and K. J. Franczyk, 233-272. Society for Sedimentary Geology, Rocky Mountain Section.

Picard, M. D. 1993. The Early Mesozoic history of Wyoming. In *Geology of Wyoming*, ed. A. W. Snoke, J. R. Steidtmann, and S. M. Roberts, 210-248. Geological Survey of Wyoming, Memoir 5.

Picard, M. D. 1997. Mesozoic history of Wyoming. In *Proceedings of the 32nd annual forum on the geology of industrial minerals*, ed. R. W. Jones and R. E. Harris, 73-106. Geological Survey of Wyoming.

Pipiringos, G. N., and R. B. O'Sullivan. 1978. *Principal unconformities in Triassic and Jurassic rocks, Western Interior United States – a preliminary survey*. Professional Paper 1035-A. Denver, CO: U.S. Geological Survey.

Ploynoi, M., and W. C. Parcell. 2005. Developing of Middle Jurassic microbial buildups in Bighorn Basin, Wyoming. *Geological Society of America Abstracts with Programs* 37: 17.

Redden, J. A., Z. E. Peterman, R. E. Zartman, and E. DeWitt. 1990. U-Th-Pb geochronology and preliminary interpretation of Precambrian tectonic events in the Black Hills, South Dakota. In *The Early Proterozoic Trans-Hudson Orogen of North America*, ed. J. F. Lewry and M. R. Stauffer, 229-251. Geological Association of Canada, Special Paper 37.

Robinson, C. S. 1956. *Geology of the Devils Tower National Monument, Wyoming*. Bulletin 1021-I. Denver, CO: U.S. Geological Survey.

Robinson, C. S. 1998. *Geology of Devils Tower National Monument, Wyoming*. Devils Tower Natural History Association.

Sabel, J. M. 1981. The sedimentology of the Spearfish Formation. MS thesis, South Dakota Schools of Mines and Technology.

Sabel, J.M. 1984. Sedimentology and depositional history of the Permo-Triassic Spearfish Formation, southwestern Black Hills, South Dakota. In *The Permian and Pennsylvanian Geology of Wyoming*, ed. J. Goolsby, and D. Morton, 295-309, 35th Annual Field Conference Guidebook. Casper, WY: Wyoming Geological Association.

Saleeby, J. B., and C. Busby-Spera. 1992. Early Mesozoic tectonic evolution of the western U.S. cordillera. In *The Cordilleran Orogen: Conterminous U.S.*, ed. B. C. Burchfiel, P. W. Lipman, and M. L. Zoback, 107-168. Geological Society of America, The Geology of North America G3.

Schmude, D. 1999. Interplay of uplift, erosion, sedimentation and preservation of Middle Jurassic rocks, Big Horn Basin, Wyoming. Bulletin 83. Tulsa, OK: American Association of Petroleum Geologists.

Steidtmann, J. R. 1993. The Cretaceous foreland basin and its sedimentary record. In *Geology of Wyoming*, ed. A. W. Snoke, J. R. Steidtmann, and S. M. Roberts, 250-271. Geological Survey of Wyoming, Memoir 5.

Steidtmann, J. R., L. T. Middleton, and M. W. Shuster. 1989. Post-Laramide (Oligocene) uplift in the Wind River Range, Wyoming. *Geology* 17: 38-41.

Strahler, A. N. 1960. Physical Geography. 2nd ed. New York: John Wiley & Sons.

Williams, M. K., and W. C. Parcell. 2003. Stratigraphic relationships within the Middle Jurassic Gypsum Spring Formation (Bajocian and Bathonian), Bighorn Basin, Wyoming and Montana. *American Association of Petroleum Geologists Annual Meeting Expanded Abstracts* 12: 181-182.

Appendix A: Geologic Map Graphic

The following page is a snapshot of the geologic map for Devils Tower National Monument. For a poster-size PDF of this map or for digital geologic map data, please see the included CD or visit the Geologic Resource Evaluation publications Web page (http://www.nature.nps.gov/geology/inventory/gre_publications.cfm).

Geologic Map of Devils Tower NM

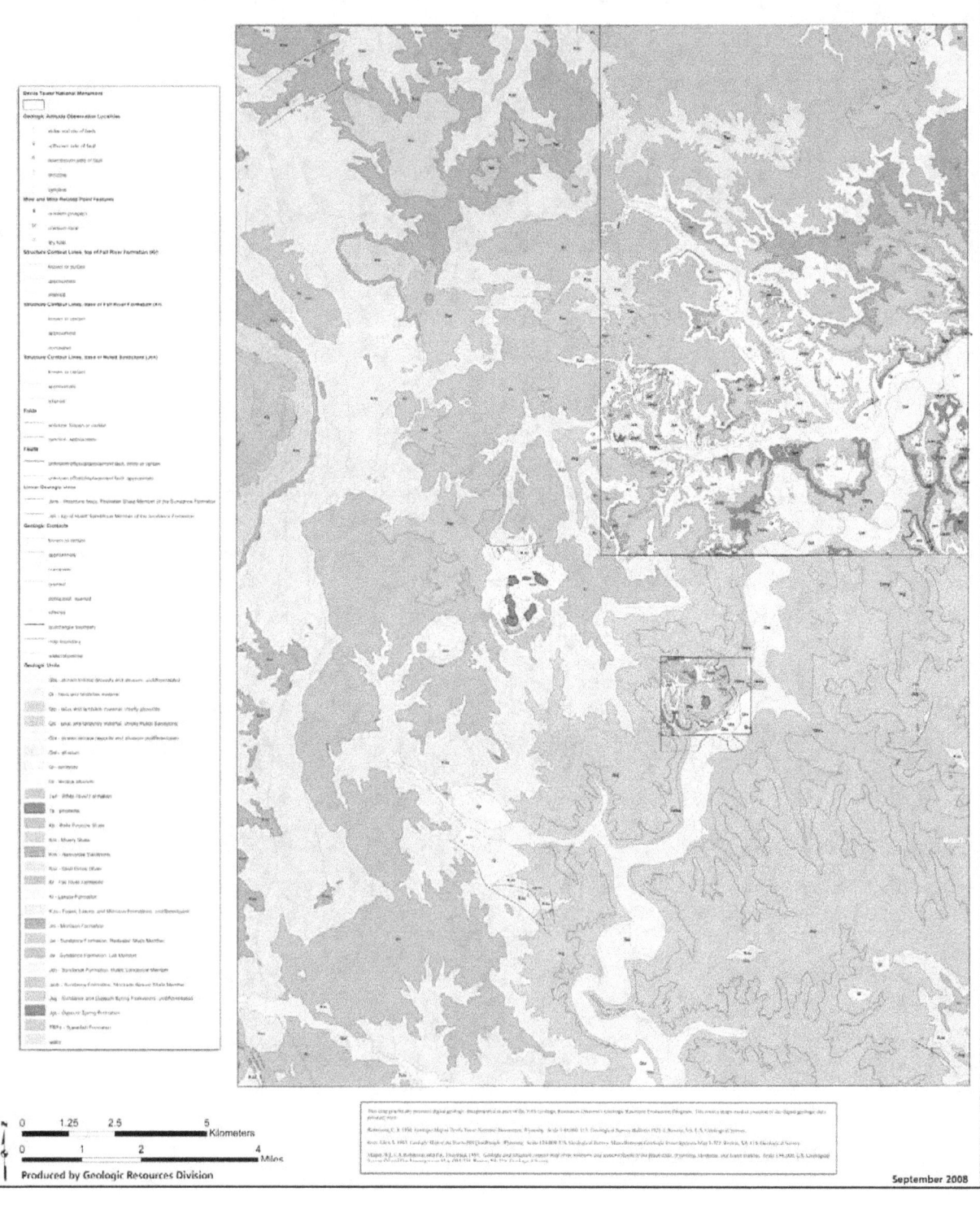

0   1.25   2.5   5
Kilometers

0   1   2   4
Miles

Produced by Geologic Resources Division

September 2008

Devils Tower National Monument
Geologic Resource Evaluation Report

Natural Resource Report NPS/NRPC/GRD/NRR—2008/046
NPS D-86, September 2008

National Park Service
Director • Mary A. Bomar

Natural Resource Stewardship and Science
Associate Director • Bert Frost

Natural Resource Program Center
The Natural Resource Program Center (NRPC) is the core of the NPS Natural Resource Stewardship and Science Directorate. The Center Director is located in Fort Collins, with staff located principally in Lakewood and Fort Collins, Colorado and in Washington, D.C. The NRPC has five divisions: Air Resources Division, Biological Resource Management Division, Environmental Quality Division, Geologic Resources Division, and Water Resources Division. NRPC also includes three offices: The Office of Education and Outreach, the Office of Inventory, Monitoring and Evaluation, and the Office of Natural Resource Information Systems. In addition, Natural Resource Web Management and Partnership Coordination are cross-cutting disciplines under the Center Director. The multidisciplinary staff of NRPC is dedicated to resolving park resource management challenges originating in and outside units of the national park system.

Geologic Resources Division
Chief • Dave Steensen
Planning Evaluation and Permits Branch Chief • Carol McCoy

Credits
Author • John Graham
Review • Rachel Benton and Carol McCoy
Editing • Thomas W. Judkins, Sid Covington, and Melanie Ransmeier
Digital Map Production • Stephanie O'Meara and Trista Thornberry-Ehrlich
Map Layout Design • Melanie Ransmeier